Disorder in the Court!

Disorder in the Court!

Bob Terrell

and

Marcellus "Buck" Buchanan

Bright Mountain Books   Asheville, North Carolina

Cover art by Gary Fields

Printed in the United States of America

ISBN: 0-914875-04-3 (hardcover)
       0-914875-05-1 (paperback)

Library of Congress Cataloging in Publication Data

Terrell, Bob.
    Disorder in the court!

    1. Courts--North Carolina--Anecdotes, facetiae,
satire, etc.   2. North Carolina--Anecdotes, facetiae,
satire, etc.   I. Buchanan, Marcellus, 1923-
II. Title.
K184.T47   1984   347.756'01   84-21483
ISBN 0-914875-04-3 347.56071
ISBN 0-914875-05-1 (pbk.)

Contents

Preface

For years we have threatened to write a book together. We are distant cousins, and we grew up in the same home town, Sylva, North Carolina. We have collected numerous stories over the years which we felt should not be lost to our people—stories of North Carolinians from the mountains to the coast, about simple folks and people in high places.

Disorder in the Court! draws heavily on our combined experiences before the bar and behind a typewriter. The courtroom is the setting for many stories, but since disorder reigns in nearly every sphere of human endeavor, we've included tales from several related areas as well. We've tried to portray the humorous side of things, but some stories which point out life's ironies or the best (or worst) of human nature seemed appropriate, too.

The courtroom can be a raw, sometimes ribald place where the dramas of life and death are acted every day. "Acted" is often the proper word, for many an act befitting a Shakespearean stage has been portrayed in the courtroom. The court is also a place where folks, as one jurist so aptly put it in this book, "let it all hang out." As you shall see, not everything that happens in the courtroom is deadly serious.

We had the cooperation of many people around the state—judges, attorneys, law-enforcement personnel, political figures—who cheerfully contributed their favorite stories to our collection. We are indebted to all, and our thanks are heartfelt.

This is not to say that all of these stories are the gospel truth. Some are simply tall tales, and you'll easily be able to distinguish which they are. We changed some names to protect the guilty and some others to avoid embarrassment, but mostly we told them just as they occurred.

This book, to be true, had to be written in the vernacular of the people who made it possible. We feel, however, that it has adequate "redeeming social value" to render it not truly offensive to those who read it in the spirit in which it was written.

Publisher's note: For clarification, the use of the personal pronoun "I" in these stories identifies Marcellus Buchanan; both authors use the third person. Stories contributed by others are usually self-evident.

Disorder in the Court!

1 • *Trial and Error*

Beware the Spoken Word

Lawyers aren't your ordinary, run-of-the-mill dummies —though some of them may sound that way at times. There must be gremlins within the souls of us all that make wrong words or senseless sentences pop out at times. Attorneys go through four years of college, law school, and then have to pass an exam to certify them to ask questions like these:

"Did you keep that in your possession all the time you had it?"

Or, questioning a witness who had just identified himself in a photograph entered into evidence: "Were you there when that picture was taken?"

"How long have you practiced surgery as a surgeon?"

"The twenty-fourth of December, you say . . . uh, was that the day before Christmas?"

Sometimes lawyers and witnesses team up for hilarious question-and-answer routines, like these:

Q: "Do you know how he was when alone?"
A: "No, sir, I was never with him when he was alone."

Q: "You say he was cruel to you? What did he do to you?"

A: "He hit me and bit me."

Q: "You say he hit you. What did he hit you with?"

A: "His fist."

Q: "What did he bite you with?"

Q: "What was he painting the inside of the drum with?"

A: "Paint."

Q: "Do you think that this is a permanent condition, doctor?"

A: "Well, it is temporarily permanent."

Q: "What would cause the pressure to be greater on one side than on the other?"

A: "Increased pressure on that side."

Q: "Were you acquainted with the decedent?"

A: "Yes, sir."

Q: "Before or after he died?"

Q: "Do you recall approximately the time that you examined the body of Mr. Smythe?"

A: "It was in the evening. The autopsy started at about 8:30 p.m."

Q. "And Mr. Smythe was dead at the time, is that correct?"

A: "No. He was sitting on the table wondering why I was doing an autopsy."

Give It Thought

Many a young attorney has learned the hard way to think through any statement he makes in the courtroom before he makes it.

A young lawyer, pleading his first case, had been retained by a farmer to prosecute a railway company for killing twenty-four of his hogs.

The young attorney wanted to impress the jury with the magnitude of the loss.

"Twenty-four hogs, ladies and gentlemen," he said. "Twenty-four hogs! Twice the number there are in this jury box!"

Solicitors and District Attorneys

The prosecuting official for the State of North Carolina has through the years been known as the "solicitor." It is a designation I* revere and it has always drawn into my thinking the one who controls and prosecutes the criminal dockets in our state. It conjures up memories of such able men as John M. Queen, Thad Bryson, and Glenn Brown, all of whom held the office and served North Carolina with distinction.

Not long ago, someone conceived the notion of enacting a statute in North Carolina authorizing the solicitors to be also known as "District Attorneys"—and allowing them to use the terms interchangeably.

Shortly after the enactment of this statute, I received a memorandum from the administrative office of the courts advising me that most solicitors had chosen the designa-

*"I" refers to Marcellus Buchanan throughout the book.

tion of district attorney, and suggesting that for the sake of uniformity we all use that title.

Seldom do I respond to memorandums, but this one was in my opinion deserving of some reply. I immediately dictated to my secretary the following reply, and I print it in its entirety:

"Receipt is acknowledged of your memorandum of July 2, 1973. Kindest regards, Marcellus Buchanan, Superior Court SOLICITOR."

One example of the reason for my choosing to be called solicitor rather than district attorney (other than the fact that it has been used in North Carolina since independence) is an episode which happened to Superior Court Judge Lacy Thornburg of Sylva.

A drunk called him at three in the morning from the Jackson County jail, asking him to come down to the jail and make his bond.

When Lacy woke up enough to realize what the man was saying, he said, "Do you realize what time it is? Why in the world if you wanted to call somebody didn't you call the solicitor?"

"Oh, my God," the man responded, "I didn't want to go THAT high!"

A Matter of Color

Ken McDaniels, a black assistant district attorney in Buncombe County, was trying a defendant for driving under the influence, and part of the evidence was that the defendant had a red face when the officer stopped him, indicating that he had been drinking.

During closing arguments, the defense attorney told the judge that the reason the defendant had a red face was due to the fact that he was wearing a red shirt and the shirt was reflecting on his face.

After the defense attorney concluded his argument, Ken rose slowly to his feet and said, "Your Honor, I have on a white shirt today. Does my face look white?"

Lawyer from Charlotte

Union County Deputy Sheriff Curtil L. Rollins served as bailiff during a 1968 criminal session of superior court in Monroe. Judge John D. McConnell of Southern Pines had summoned the bailiff to the bench for a short consultation when an inmate, finding the courtroom lockup door had been left insecure, opened the door, sped across the courtroom, jumped the rail, and went out the back door. Rollins and other court officials gave chase.

As the fleeing escapee neared the door that would admit him to the stairway to the first floor and ultimately to freedom, an official of the court came through the door, and seeing the running man, politely held the door open for him while he sped through.

After a chase through the courthouse, the escapee was apprehended and returned to the lockup. Judge McConnell called the court official who had held the door open before the bench and asked him what prompted him to be so nice to an escapee.

"I'm sorry, Your Honor," said the official. "I didn't realize he was an inmate. He looked like a lawyer from Charlotte to me."

A Few Days Make a Difference

A few years ago I held a two-weeks' session of criminal court in Haywood County. The county provided parking spaces behind the courthouse for the judge and the solicitor. I had a habit of leaving my keys in the ignition switch, and on Wednesday of my first court week I left the courthouse in the afternoon and found my parking place empty. My car was gone!

I reported the theft to Sheriff Jack Arrington, and the next day his deputies found my car abandoned in the Haywood County town of Clyde, where obviously some joy-riders had left it when it ran out of gas. The car was not damaged, and I gave it no further thought.

It so happened, though, that on the day of the theft, a young man had entered a plea of guilty to car theft in my court and the judge had put him in jail awaiting sentencing the next day.

When I arrived at the courthouse the next morning, the jailer brought a hand-scrawled note to me from the young man in the jail. The note read: "Dear Mr. Solicitor: I heerd about your car getting stold yesterday. Please wait a few more days to sentence me, cause I would rather walk through hell doused in lighter fluid than to come up before you today."

I waited in accordance with his request, showed the judge his note, and because of the belly laugh the judge got out of the incident, he put the young man on probation.

6

Dead or Alive!

Some said John M. Queen, the fabled solicitor of North Carolina's old Twentieth (now the Thirtieth) Judicial District, had eyes in the back of his totally bald head.

He had a habit of keeping all defendants in the courtroom until their cases were called—and if any defendant left the courtroom for any reason, Queen would call that man's case, have him called out, and a capias issued.

One afternoon toward the middle of a busy court week, an old gentleman charged with making good liquor and selling it to good men was waiting for his trial to come up. About three o'clock, the old fellow was bound and compelled to answer a call of nature, so he eased out of his seat and tip-toed out the back of the courtroom.

As the old man went down the stairs toward the men's room, John Queen called his case, and when the man didn't answer, Queen asked the sheriff to "call him out." When the sheriff called and the defendant did not respond, the judge ordered "judgment nisi on his bond and an instanter capias for his arrest."

Old Jim Turpin, hearing his friend called out, dashed out of the courtroom, ran down the stairs, burst into the men's room, and grabbed the startled old moonshiner by the shoulders.

"Fer God's sake," Jim shouted, "get up yander to the courtroom as fast as you can. John Queen's done had you called and failed, ni sci'd, sci fa'd, and the judge has ordered a bench-legged warrant for you—AND THAT MEANS DEAD OR ALIVE!"

Tell Me How

Asheville Attorney Joe Reynolds defended a mountain fellow against a charge of assault with a deadly weapon in Buncombe County Superior Court. Evidence showed that the man had stabbed a cab driver in Asheville with a pocket knife.

Under oath, the man revealed that he had gone to North Lexington Avenue and "took up" with a couple of gals who lived by the world's oldest profession.

"While I was a-whoring around," the fellow said, "I tried to drink all the bars dry."

"How many bars?" he was asked.

"Ever' one I could find," he answered. "Must've been eight or ten."

Then the fellow called a taxi and told the driver to take him home. The driver knew him and knew he ought to be home, so he set a bee-line course toward the man's house.

"Why did you stab him?" the prosecuting attorney asked.

"I tol' him to stop."

"And?"

"He didn't stop."

"So you stabbed him because he didn't stop?"

" 'At's right."

"Why?"

" 'Cause I tol' him to."

"Wait a minute," the judge broke in. "Let me get this straight." He looked at the defendant. "You say you are sixty-eight years old?"

" 'At's right, Your Honor."

"And you spent the day on Lexington Avenue chasing whores and drinking liquor?"

"An' part of the night," the man corrected.

"Before we go any further," the judge said, banging his gavel, "I'm going to recess this court for an hour."

He looked again at the defendant. "Sir," he said, "you are about my age. Would you come back to my chambers and talk to me? I want to learn your secret."

Room for Doubt

I once had one of the finest assistant solicitors in the state in Jimmy Howell, who lived in Haywood County. He was meticulously thorough, hung onto a case like a bulldog, and hated more than anything else in the world to take a dismissal in any case.

I can recall only one voluntary dismissal he took. While calling the calendar one morning he came to a particular name and when he called it the sheriff spoke up, "Mr. Solicitor, that man died last night."

Jimmy cast the sheriff an aggravated look. "Have you seen the body, sheriff?"

"No, sir, I haven't," the sheriff replied, "but I have it on good authority that he is dead."

So, after thinking it over, Howell took a "dismissal with leave to reopen."

Get On with the Evidence

The defendant was being tried on charges of making bootleg liquor. The district attorney read the warrant in open court and asked him how he intended to plead.

"I don't know, Your Honor," the defendant replied. "I ain't heard the evidence yet."

9

Bad Enough Trouble

Testimony went about as Attorney Bob Swain of Asheville expected. The charge of rape against his client was indeed a serious accusation, but he was convinced that the young man was innocent, and the flow of testimony so far suited the purposes of defense.

The defendant had told Swain that the sexual act between himself and the young woman had been a friendly thing, with no force involved, and Swain had believed him.

Testimony in district court had established that the young man, an air-conditioning mechanic from a small mountain town, had come to Asheville with a male friend for a weekend. They met two girls, one of whom was now the plaintiff, and had taken them to a tavern on the edge of town where they drank and danced for a while. Then they motored across town to another place where they partied some more.

Leaving the second place, the mechanic and his date drove the other couple to the other girl's house and dropped them off, then drove back to an isolated spot, parked, turned on the radio, and listened to music. One thing led to another and soon the girl's clothing was piled neatly in the back seat of the car, and the couple, in the front seat, let nature take its course.

Under oath, the girl said that the mechanic forced her to have sexual intercourse with him.

Questioning her, Swain asked, "Is it not true, young lady, that you took off your own clothes?"

"Yes," she said. "I took them off rather than having them torn off."

"And is it not also true that you folded them in a neat

pile and put them in the back seat?"

"Yes, I did," she said. "I didn't see no sense in getting them messed up."

"And isn't it true," Swain pressed, "that you and the defendant had sex in the front seat not once, but several times?"

"Yes."

The judge leaned forward and asked, "What do you mean? Explain that, please."

"Well," she said, searching for the right words, "we had sex, and then he got out of the car and went to the bathroom, and then we had sex again, and I got out and went to the bathroom, and when I came back we resumed."

"Resumed?" the judge asked.

"You know," she said. "We had sex again."

The judge's eyebrows raised, and he cast an admiring glance at the defendant.

"Now, young lady," Swain said, "were you really afraid? I mean, *really* afraid?"

"Yes," she said. "He threatened me."

"You didn't try to shout for help?"

"I didn't see anybody around."

"Did you see a house nearby with lights on?"

"Yes, but there wasn't but one."

"When he got out of the car," Swain said, "or when you got out of the car, why didn't you run to the house and shout for help?"

"I was afraid he'd catch me," she said, "and hurt me."

"You said you didn't have anything on."

"That's right, I didn't."

"Then there was nothing to impede your running?"

"No, sir."

"What did the defendant have on?"

"He had his clothes on."

"Did he still have his trousers on?"

"They were down around his ankles."

"Are you telling this court," Swain asked, "that you didn't think you could outrun him to the house when you didn't have anything on and he had his pants down around his ankles? You don't really think you could have outrun him?"

"Depends," she said slowly, "on how fast you run."

"All right, young lady," Swain said, "when you had sex, exactly what was your position?"

"Lying across the front seat," she said.

"Which way was your head?"

"Toward the steering wheel."

"There wasn't much room, I take it," Swain said.

"No, sir, not much."

"Was the car door open?"

"Yes, sir."

"Do you know about the little dome light in the car," he asked, "the one that comes on when the door opens? Was it on?"

"No, sir."

"Was it burned out?"

"No, sir."

"Isn't it true, young lady," Swain asked in his sternest voice, "that you lay there with your finger on that little button in the door, the one that holds that dome light off? Isn't it true that the light wasn't on because you held the button that kept it off?"

"Yes," she said, "but it flickered a few times."

By this time the judge was having difficulty keeping a straight face. No one else in the courtroom was trying.

Snickers and guffaws came from the occupied seats.

"Young lady," Swain said, "will you please tell this court why you kept your finger on that switch while a man allegedly raped you repeatedly?"

"No need in getting anybody else involved," she said, feeling her case slipping away. "I was in bad enough trouble myself."

The judge could stand it no longer. He stopped testimony at that point and threw the case out of court.

Next Best Thing

An Asheville attorney, famous as a shrewd cross-examiner, questioned a witness in an assault case in which his client was the accused. The attorney maneuvered the fellow into admitting that he hadn't actually seen the offense committed.

"So," the attorney boomed, "you say you didn't actually see the defendant bite off this man's ear?"

"No, I didn't see him bite it off," the witness said, "I just seen him spit it out."

Who's Driving?

Charles Hipps of Waynesville, a distinguished attorney, was one of the first assistant solicitors I hired when I took office in 1967. He was a superb trial lawyer, and one of the finest men who ever worked for my organization.

During a court session in Jackson County in the trial of a rather complicated breaking and entering case that had been investigated by a member of the State Bureau of

Investigation, the SBI agent became a problem: He thought he knew more about the trial preparation and the order of presentation of evidence than Charles Hipps.

We were unable to convince him that Hipps knew how his case should be presented, in what order, what evidence should be put before the jury, and what should not. We had numerous recesses, and at each recess the SBI agent would approach Charles and give him unsolicited advice.

Finally, Charles reached the breaking point. I was standing near when the agent offered too much advice, and Charles threw back his head, looked the agent in the eye, and said, "Why don't you just load the wagon, and I'll drive the team."

Who, Indeed?

Dr. H. F. "Cotton" Robinson, retired chancellor of Western Carolina University, sought counsel in defense of a suit filed against the university during his tenure, and settled upon Asheville Attorney Herbert L. Hyde, an alumnus of the university.

In the courtroom, Hyde, the lone legal representative of the university, matched wits—and evidence—against two attorneys for the other side.

At the end of the first day of testimony, Dr. Robinson asked Hyde to dinner, and their conversation, quite naturally, got around to the trial.

"How do you think we're doing?" Dr. Robinson asked.

"Oh, we're doing all right," Hyde said. "I think we did just fine today."

"Tomorrow," Dr. Robinson said, "I would like you to

have help. Bring another lawyer."

"Another lawyer?" Hyde said, puzzled. "Why? We did all right today."

"Maybe," said Dr. Robinson, vaguely.

"All right, Chancellor," Hyde said, "out with it. What's bothering you?"

"Well, I had a thought sitting there today," Dr. Robinson said, "that we could have done even better."

"How?"

"I noticed how those two lawyers on the other side worked together," Dr. Robinson said.

"And?"

"Well, it seemed to me," said Dr. Robinson, "that while one of them was standing up talking, the other was sitting there thinking."

"Yes?"

"And when you were up talking," Dr. Robinson concluded, "we didn't have anybody thinking for us!"

A Valid Excuse

A hard-working superior court jury in McDowell County disposed of seven tough cases in a five-day court week, and at three o'clock on Friday afternoon, the judge thanked the jury, told the members they could have the remainder of the afternoon off, mentioned that their checks for jury service would be mailed immediately, and added that if any juror needed a written statement for his employer about his jury service, that that juror could ask the clerk of court to verify on a certain form his service during the week.

As the jury filed out, one of the jurors approached the

bench.

"Judge," he asked, "can I get a written excuse to show my wife?"

The judge said yes, the clerk filled out the form, and the man folded it and placed it in his coat pocket and went happily out of the courthouse.

No Whales Here

Several years ago I tried a defendant in rural, mountainous Graham County who had been charged with larceny of a heifer calf, tan and white, of a value of approximately six hundred dollars.

The judge, from Eastern North Carolina, was probably one of the most picayune judges who ever sat on a superior court bench in North Carolina.

He was extremely particular about how the charges were worded in the bills of indictment presented in his court. I had in my bill of indictment precisely described the heifer calf by color and by weight, and there was absolutely nothing wrong with the description.

However, the judge called me to the bench, and pointing to the bill of indictment said to me, "Mr. Solicitor, I am disturbed about this bill of indictment. It does not appear to describe this calf sufficiently, because, as you probably know, whales have calves."

I was astounded. I replied, "Judge, to be perfectly frank with you, I have never seen nor heard of a whale calf in Graham County—and neither has anybody on that jury."

I don't know whether it was because he was so particular or because he became angered at my remarks, but he required me to send another bill of indictment stating that the calf was of the bovine species.

Just How Much?

A federal judge, holding court in Asheville and seeing a familiar face come before the bar of justice for moonshining, asked the defendant, "Sam, how many times have you come before me for making illegal whiskey?"

"I don't rightly recollect, Your Honor."

"Have you made whiskey all your life?"

"Reckon so, Your Honor."

"How much whiskey do you think you've made, Sam?"

"I don't rightly know, Your Honor."

"Do you think you've made enough to fill this courtroom?"

Sam let his eye roam from wall to wall and ceiling to floor, silently measuring.

"I doubt it, Judge," he said, "but I've made enough to make 'er slosh!"

Affirmative Gesture

Once in New Hanover County Superior Court, during some preposterous testimony of a defendant in a carrying-a-concealed-weapon-and-trespassing case, the judge interrupted the testimony and said to the court, "If any of you believe this story, stand on your heads."

When the judge looked back around, the defendant had stepped down from the witness stand and was standing on his head in front of the entire court.

The Guilty Drunks

Judge Sam J. Ervin III, son of Senator Sam and now a member of the United States Circuit Court of Appeals, once held superior court with me in Murphy. The Cherokee County courthouse there is the only one in North Carolina constructed of solid marble, the marble being quarried within ten miles of the building.

Judge Ervin lived in Morganton, about two hundred miles from Murphy, but decided he would wait until Monday morning to make the drive. He would get an early start and be in Murphy in time to open court at ten o'clock.

Fate plays funny tricks on all of us—even superior court judges. That morning the fog was so heavy that traffic was slowed to a snail's pace. Judge Ervin could only inch along, and consequently was an hour and a half late reaching Murphy.

I got to the courthouse around nine and took my seat at the solicitor's table. Checking over my calendar, I found I had twenty-five drunk drivers on for jury trial—and not a single plea of guilty.

Around nine-thirty I knew Judge Ervin was going to be extremely late because of the fog, and having to try twenty-five drunks would shoot holes in our whole week's schedule, so I decided to offer them an out.

I turned to the defendants and announced that if they wanted to remand their cases to the district court and pay off their fines, this judge would let them do it rather than have to try them, and they wouldn't risk active prison sentences.

Not a single one accepted my offer.

The judge's chambers were just off the main courtroom,

and there was an extension telephone from the clerk's office in the judge's chambers, so calls could be transferred from the clerk's office to the judge simply by punching a button.

Thinking of that telephone, I decided to try a bit of trickery to see if I couldn't convince some of those drunk drivers to accept the offer I had made. I arranged for Sheriff Blaine Stalcup to come to the courtroom, and then for the clerk to ring the judge's telephone.

When it rang, I walked across the courtroom, opened the door to the judge's chambers, left it open, and answered the phone.

"Hello . . . Yes, Judge Ervin. . . ." Everyone in the courtroom could hear me conducting a conversation that none of the defendants knew was one-sided. "Where are you calling from, sir? . . . Nantahala Gorge? . . ." I paused longer here, as if the judge were telling me a long story. "Good Lord! Are you hurt? . . . Thank God for that. . . . A drunk, you say. Well, don't let him leave. Don't let him throw that bottle away. . . . Yes, sir. . . . Yes, sir. . . . I'll get the sheriff out there right away."

I hung up, went to the door, and yelled to Sheriff Stalcup, "Blaine, Judge Ervin has just been hit by a drunk driver in Nantahala Gorge. He's not hurt, but his car's totaled. Get out there as quick as you can and bring the judge on in. He's got the drunk who hit him."

Stalcup bolted out of the courtroom, and I returned to my seat at the solicitor's desk.

In a few moments I felt a timid tap on my shoulder. I looked around and all twenty-five defendants were lined up in single file. The one at the head of the line said, "Sir, if it ain't too late, we'd like to sign them remands and get the hell out of here."

Hastily, the clerk and I took their remands and their fines, and told them how lucky they were to be getting out that easy.

The judge arrived about eleven-thirty and was astonished to see the stack of remands on his desk, which he quickly signed.

"Buck," he said to me, "I've never held a court in which *every* drunk driver paid off before court even opened."

When finally I got up enough nerve to tell Judge Ervin what I had done, he laughed heartily, and during the remainder of his six-months' rotation in my district, he made it a practice of calling me on Sunday and asking how late I wanted him to be on Monday morning.

Know the Answer

One of the first things I learned when I started practicing law in 1949 was this: Never ask your witness a question unless you know in advance what his answer will be. On cross-examination this rule does not apply—but I would always advise a young lawyer to follow the rule with his own witnesses.

A lawyer did not follow it in a local case in which a young lady brought suit against a realtor for selling her some land upon which there were judgments and liens.

She had as one of her witnesses another local real estate agent who testified as to the encumbrances on the land, and then was cross-examined by the defendant realtor's lawyer.

"Now, Mr. Smith," the attorney said, "you have been in the real estate business here along with my client for more than twenty years, haven't you?"

"Yes, I have."

"And you have been associated with him during this period of time in many, many transactions, haven't you?"

"Yes, I have—perhaps more than a hundred."

"And you, of course, are familiar with his general character and reputation as you know it to be?"

"Yes, I am."

"And what is that?"

"It is BAD!"

The lawyer was dumbfounded. At this stage, already hurt by the answer, prudence and good judgment told the lawyer to inquire no further, since it was, or should have been, obvious to him that the witness was hostile and certainly was not fond of his client.

But the lawyer, thinking he must undo some of the damage, inquired further, "What do you mean by that, Mr. Smith, and on what do you base such an opinion?"

"I base my opinion on the fact," said Mr. Smith, "that he has defrauded countless other people just like he did this lady."

And at that point, the defendant's ship slid slowly under the water and disappeared.

A Question of Where?

Troy Toppin of Edenton, sheriff of Chowan County, said a defendant named Joe was on trial in district court of Chowan County on charges of non-support of three illegitimate children.

The plaintiff, Mabel, testified that she and Joe had lived together for some time, but that Joe had left her and that she needed money to help support her three children.

"Were all your children born out of wedlock?" the judge asked.

"Oh, no, Your Honor," Mabel replied. "Two of 'em was born in Martin County."

Slip of the Mind

Many a defendant has gone free because of a slight slip of a judge's memory.

An Ashevillean named Frank Wade asked Attorney Joe Reynolds to defend him against a minor drinking charge.

Reynolds always checks for criminal records of his clients, and when he checked on Wade, he discovered a record as long as his arm, liberally sprinkled with almost every crime known to man.

Reynolds took the case, but deep in his mind he thought that Wade didn't have much of a chance, unless he could come up with something new and compelling.

Naturally, the prosecution asked Wade if he had a criminal record.

"Yes, sir," Wade said, "they might be a thing or two agin' me."

"What have you been convicted of?" the prosecutor asked.

"Nothing but some drivin'-under-the-influences," Wade said, "and I believe one breaking-and-entering. But that was a long time ago."

"Mr. Wade," the prosecutor said, moving in to make the kill, "isn't it true that you have been convicted of sixty-four charges ranging from this to that to whatever?"

"Oh, no," said Wade, shrinking in mock fear. "That wasn't me. That's another Frank Wade. They've got things so screwed up in that records office that a man can't get a fair shake."

Reynolds began to shrink, too. He knew that Wade was lying through his teeth.

"And that ain't all," Wade said in consternation. "That clerk in the records office is a bigger alcoholic than I am. He can't keep nothing straight."

"I remember that," the judge came suddenly alert. "I remember that other Frank Wade. I tried him myself."

Reynolds never knew what the judge was thinking of. All he knew was that his client walked out of the courtroom scot-free, and grinning like the cat that swallowed the canary.

Street Corner Evidence

Before the integrated court system was introduced in North Carolina, we had a literal hodge-podge of courts. Superior court was the court of general jurisdiction in which most cases were actually tried. We also had county court, municipal or city court, township courts, and justice of the peace courts. One of the problems was keeping qualified judges on the benches.

We had a judge of county court in my district who held office for eight years, trying mostly criminal cases, and it could have been said—and probably was—that he was not one of the more qualified judges.

In my law practice I once represented a defendant charged with participating in a gambling operation in the county. All of the evidence presented by the state would have led a jury to believe that my defendant was not within a half-mile of where the game was, but unfortunately there was no jury, only this judge.

When the state finished presenting its evidence, I moved for a judgment of non-suit, which meant that I wanted the case dismissed for total lack of evidence against my client.

A judge, like a jury, is supposed to determine the guilt or innocence of a defendant from evidence presented under oath from the witness stand, and is required to dismiss from his mind anything that he might have heard about the case or might have read about it.

Upon hearing my motion for non-suit, however, this judge looked at me and said, "Well, I can see where the evidence might be weak in this case, but in view of all I have heard around town and on the street, I'm going to find him guilty."

Jury Selection

In his years as district attorney of the 27-A Solicitorial District in Gastonia, Joseph G. Brown has learned at least two things about jury selection: (1) many people will do almost anything to get off a jury, and (2) the process of selecting a jury produces a lot of humor.

During selection of a jury for a defendant charged with assault on a female, Brown asked whether any member of the jury panel had ever been charged with the offense of assault on a female.

Three members of the panel held up their hands and Brown immediately excused them. Another male member raised his hand and asked if he could say something to the district attorney.

Given permission, he said, "Mr. Brown, I have never laid a hand on my wife, but if you will excuse me from this jury, I promise I'll whip her as soon as I get home."

Prosecuting a murder case that had been given an inordinate amount of newspaper and television publicity, Brown asked the jury panel if anyone had read about the case in the newspapers or seen the news of the case on television, and whether they had formed or expressed an opinion based on what they had read or heard on the news.

After asking that question of the first five jurors, Brown asked the sixth.

"No, sir," the juror replied, "I have not read or heard anything in the media about this case, but my wife has— and if you'd like, I'll be glad to give you her opinion."

A standard question for a jury panel is whether any of the attorneys participating in the case has ever appeared in a trial in which anyone on the jury had an interest.

Grady Stott, a Gastonia attorney, asked that question of a jury panel and a man held up his hand.

"Mr. Stott, you represented my wife in our divorce case," the juror said.

"Sir," Grady said, "would you state whether or not I did anything during the course of that trial which might prejudice you in the case we are about to try?"

"No, Mr. Stott," the juror replied, "you lost the case."

Early Birds

People who live in Clay County in the far western end of North Carolina are early risers. They believe in getting up early and getting things done. Because of that, Judge Felix E. Alley, Jr., of Waynesville, and I held a memorable day of court a few years ago.

When the district court system was established in North Carolina in 1967 for the trial of misdemeanor cases, Judge Alley, known to his friends as Gene Alley, was elected as one of the first three judges in the Thirtieth Judicial District. Gene Alley was probably one of the most brilliant lawyers ever reared in Western North Carolina; he was indeed a "student of the law." He also possessed a great portion of what we in the mountains call "common horse sense."

Soon after he was elected to the district court bench, we were scheduled to hold court in Clay County. Hayesville, Clay's county seat, was some ninety miles west of Waynesville, Judge Alley's home, so he and I drove to Hayesville on Sunday, spent the night, and were on the spot to hold court on Monday morning as scheduled.

Clay County is not one of the crime centers of North Carolina. Normally our court load would consist of eight or ten cases, most of them traffic cases.

Monday morning, with court scheduled to begin at nine-thirty, Gene and I left our motel at seven-thirty and walked to the courthouse before daylight. The janitor had the courthouse doors unlocked and we walked through the building, turning on lights, and made our way to the courtroom.

About seven forty-five it was daylight and I looked out the window of the courtroom and saw about a dozen men congregated in front of Phillips Store. I knew within reason that those were the defendants on our calendar, so I raised the window and hollered to them, "Boys, if you want to come on up, we'll hear your cases and let you get on about your work."

In a few minutes they trooped into the courtroom. I had a copy of the calendar which told what each defendant was charged with, but since the clerk's office had not yet opened I had none of the case jackets containing the particulars.

Judge Alley was on the bench in his robe. I told him, "Why don't we go ahead and see how far we can get without the case jackets?"

He told me to call the first case. The defendant pleaded guilty, paid his fine and the costs, and left. One by one, the defendants followed suit until all had pleaded guilty and each case had been disposed.

Judge Alley then said, "Buck, have we got anything else to do?"

I said, "No, Your Honor, we're all finished."

"Then, why don't we hit the road."

The clerk's office still wasn't open when we passed by. We got in my car and left, and that's the only time during all my years as solicitor that we convened court and concluded court before time to open court.

How Much Rain?

Attorneys and their clients pay special attention to how they phrase certain statements. As in writing, what really counts is how you string the words together!

Frank Wade went to his favorite attorney, Asheville's Joe

Reynolds, and asked Reynolds to file suit against an Asheville dentist for doing some work on adjacent property that caused Wade's basement to flood.

Reynolds checked the weather records for the date in question, just to make sure he wouldn't be surprised with anything in court. The weather records showed that 1.75 inches of rain fell in Asheville that day, the most rain in a long time, certainly enough to flood most basements in town.

Reynolds went to the offices of *The Asheville Citizen-Times* and looked up the paper for that date in the microfilm files. A front-page story carried the news of the 1.75 inches of rain that fell in Asheville and an amazing 8.0 inches that fell in Hendersonville. A huge picture on the front page showed floodwaters in Hendersonville.

During the trial, Frank took the stand, and the defense attorney quizzed him at length about weather conditions on the day in question.

"It was a mite damp," Wade said, "best I remember."

"Best you remember!" the defense exploded, and began wagging a copy of *The Asheville Citizen* for that date before the jury. "Best he remembers! Ladies and gentlemen of the jury, *The Asheville Citizen* says it rained eight inches that day! Eight inches! That's enough to flood the country. The flooding of Mr. Wade's basement was an Act of God!"

" 'Twasn't, either," said Wade calmly, and the jury and defense attorney stared at him with open mouths. "It rained eight inches in Hendersonville," Wade said. "It only rained one and three-quarter inches here!"

Reynolds thought, "By golly, I couldn't have phrased that better myself!"

Although 1.75 inches of rain is a frog-strangler, beside 8.0 inches it's only a drop or two.

The members of the jury passed the newspaper around, shook their heads when they noted that "only 1.75 inches" of rain fell in Asheville that day—and awarded Frank Wade their unanimous decision.

Turn About

A defendant, brought to court from the jail in Wilmington, would not divulge his name. To all inquiries he answered that his name was "John Doe."

He was returned to jail and brought again the next day to face a different judge.

When the judge learned of the defendant's refusal to tell his name the previous day, he answered the defendant's request for a court-appointed attorney with this response:

"All right, the court will appoint an attorney for you," and, with a twinkle in his eye, added, "His name is John Doe."

Amplification

In 1976 Macon County built a new county office building that included courtroom facilities. It replaced an old red brick building that had been heated by pot-bellied stoves in all the offices as well as in the courtroom.

I normally speak in a rather loud voice and seldom use an amplification system, even if one is provided in the courtroom.

The new Macon County courtroom was extremely modern and equipped with a very sensitive amplification system with microphones at all of the desks, the witness stand, the court reporter's box, and wherever else amplification was needed.

The first time I held court in the new room, the judge was Lacy Thornburg of Sylva. I started with the call of the calendar, calling the names of all the defendants to see if they were present and what their pleas were. We had a rather lengthy calendar at that session and I had been calling names for about twenty minutes when a lawyer from Sylva named Phil Haire, who was formerly a law partner of Judge Thornburg's, walked in, went straight to the judge's bench, put his elbows on the bench, and began talking to the judge.

One of my assistant solicitors was sitting at the table with me, and a microphone was between us. Since I usually switch off the microphones at my desk, I thought this one was off—but it wasn't.

I leaned over to my assistant, aggravated at being interrupted, and said in a rather low voice, "John, if that ignorant son of a bitch would let the judge alone, I'd finish the call of the calendar."

That certainly was a sensitive mike—and it wasn't more than six inches from my face. It boomed my voice through the courtroom, and when the people in the room finished laughing, Judge Thornburg, wiping tears of laughter off his face, said to Phil Haire, "You heard what the gentleman said, Phil; you'd better just wait and talk to me at recess."

Strangest Case

One of the strangest cases to come before Judge E. Maurice Braswell was in Southport, Brunswick County, in

1964. The case concerned non-support of an illegitimate child. The child was in the courtroom, along with its mother and neighbors.

Earlier, on the defendant's motion, there had been a blood-grouping test made by a physician in Wilmington.

At the appropriate time, Solicitor Bowman called the doctor as a state's witness. During the doctor's testimony, the solicitor asked, "Now, doctor, based on your medical knowledge and the blood-grouping test which you performed, do you have an opinion satisfactory to yourself whether the defendant could be the father of this child over here?"

"Yes, sir," said the doctor, and after a pause he added, "but I also have an opinion that the mother isn't the mother."

Pandemonium broke loose in the courtroom. The professed mother went into hysterics, and before long everyone in the audience seemed to be taking sides. Judge Braswell had to recess court for a lengthy period of time, and upon returning, he declared a mistrial.

"Although I did not get to retry the case," Judge Braswell said, "having rotated to another district, I later asked Solicitor Bowman what happened next, and Bowman said, 'The doctor was so upset by the mother's reaction in the courtroom that he voluntarily redid the blood-grouping test and found out that the mother could have been the mother after all (and was in truth the mother) whereupon the defendant decided it was in his best interest to plead guilty, which he did—and that ended the whole thing.' "

He Missed!

In New Hanover Superior Court one morning, the bailiff took a standing position behind the defendant, and rested his hand on his own holstered gun.

Glancing around the courtroom, the bailiff let his mind wander. The defendant, sitting at the table, suddenly slammed both hands on the top of the table in a gesture of futility, making a noise as loud as a gunshot.

Jerked back to reality, the shocked bailiff, who had almost jumped out of his skin, looked downward to see if he had shot himself in the foot.

The Vernacular

Sometimes, inadvertently, the court becomes entangled in vernacular.

Two fine-looking young black men appeared in my court and entered pleas of guilty to racing on the highways.

They had one of the finest lawyers in the district who proceeded to make a stirring talk to the judge for lenience in view of their total lack of criminal record, their ages, and the support they were getting from their families.

"Your Honor," the lawyer said, "their mothers are here in this courtroom hoping you will let them take their sons home. These boys have learned their lesson and you will never see them in your court again if you will grant them probation on this sentence."

Wanting to see for himself, the judge said, "Well, let the mothers stand up."

Whereupon both defendants promptly stood.

Pass the Cornbread, Please

The late Henry Fisher, a trial lawyer with the Buncombe County bar, had been employed by a woman to privately prosecute a bastardy lawsuit. His client was no beauty queen; she could be described only as "ugly."

On the other side, the defendant was married to a beautiful woman.

Throughout the lawsuit, the defense attorney kept asking the jury by innuendo why a man with such a pretty wife would go out with such an ugly woman.

At closing arguments, the defense attorney told the jury, "Ladies and gentlemen, I do not like to criticize people, but in this case I feel that I must. I want you to look at the plaintiff, and I am sure that you will agree with me that she is an extremely ugly woman."

The jury looked, and two of the men nodded their heads in silent affirmation.

"Now," said the defense attorney, quite pleased with himself for scoring so delicate a point, "I want you to look at the defendant's wife. I am sure you will agree that she is a very beautiful woman."

The same two jurors nodded again.

"When you go back to the jury room," the defense attorney said, "I want you to ask yourselves this question: 'Why would a man with such a pretty wife go out with such an ugly woman?' "

The attorney sat down, his final argument finished, confident that not even Henry Fisher could sway that jury from the contrast he had wrought. But old Henry strode to the jury box, looked each juror squarely in the eye, and in his deep voice said, "Ladies and gentlemen, I am going to tell you one thing only. A man who has chocolate cake every night of the week gets a hankering every now and then for a little cornbread."

Who Is Which, or Whom?

A young man was once tried for rape before Judge Hugh Campbell in Jackson County.

Testimony spun a tangled web among the victim and the accused and the accused's wife—visits in the home, camping trips together, other weekend holidays, inseparable days of companionship.

Judge Campbell, figuring the jury must be as confused as he was, stopped the proceedings and called all counsel to the bench.

"For God's sake," the judge demanded, "will somebody tell me who is the rapor and who is the rapee?!"

That Ain't the Man!

In Wake County District Court, Sidney S. Eagles, Jr., once represented a man by court appointment on a charge of armed robbery. The defendant insisted that the witnesses against him would not show up.

On court day, Eagles asked his client to look around the courtroom and see if any of the witnesses were there. They were not, he said.

Eagles approached the district attorney and reminded him that the case had been called. "Since no witnesses have shown up," Eagles said, "and since not any are likely to, you should either dismiss the case and let us go home, or produce your witnesses and try the case."

The district attorney said there was no basis to assume that the witnesses would not be there, and then tried to engage Eagles in conversation about a plea. Eagles assured the D.A. that they were not interested in a plea, certainly not as long as no witnesses were present.

Another hour passed, a second calendar call was made, and the district attorney once again inquired of the gathered crowd whether the witnesses in this case were present, and no one answered.

Eagles pressed again for dismissal, but the D.A. declined.

Thirty minutes later the D.A. queried the crowd again for the missing witnesses, and to Eagles' surprise an elderly man raised his hand and slowly walked to the prosecutor's table.

The district attorney flashed a triumphant grin toward Eagles and called the case.

As the charge was being read and plea entered, his client frantically tugged at Eagles' coat sleeve. Eagles shook him off, paying attention to the reading of the charge. When they sat down, however, the client whispered in Eagles' ear, "That ain't the man!"

"What?" Eagles asked.

"That ain't the man!" the defendant said again.

By this time the district attorney had the man on the stand and was questioning him.

"Do you know the defendant, John Smith, seated over there?" He pointed toward Eagles' client.

"No, sir," said the witness.

The D.A. was taken aback, but he recovered quickly. Carefully he phrased the next question. "Don't you recognize the defendant, John Smith, sitting there, as the person who held you up and took your gold watch."

Eagles objected on the basis that the witness had already answered the question. The judge permitted him to answer, and he again said, "No, sir."

Intense frustration crossed the prosecutor's face and he asked, "Isn't that the man who held you up on the night of April thirteenth and robbed you?"

Over objection the man answered, "That ain't the man!" Eagles withdrew his objection.

To all further attempts to ask questions of identification of his client Eagles objected, and the court sustained the objections.

In frustration, the district attorney rested his case. Eagles had no questions for the witness, and the presiding judge, Stafford Bulluck, found the defendant not guilty.

Later inquiries by Eagles indicated that the witness had in fact been robbed but not on the occasion for which his client was accused of robbery; hence the explanations of both defendant and witness: "That ain't the man!"

Improper Equipment

Kenneth Whittington, chief of the Manteo Police Department in the early 1970s, arrested a man for indecent exposure. The case was called in Dare County District Court by Assistant Solicitor Tom Watts before Chief District Judge Fentress T. Horner.

The defendant entered a plea of not guilty.

Under direct examination by the solicitor, Chief Whittington testified that on the preceding Saturday night he had been parked in his patrol car in front of the Pioneer Theatre in downtown Manteo when he observed the accused come from the front door of the Village Tavern, a beer hall located about one hundred and fifty feet up the street.

The chief said that the accused made his way to the corner of the tavern building, stepped a few feet away from the sidewalk beside the building, and proceeded to relieve himself against the tavern building.

Chief Whittington said he arrested the man as he started to go back inside the tavern for another round.

The defendant, not represented by an attorney, told the judge that he did not want to cross-examine the state's witness, but that he did desire to tell his side of the story.

Being duly sworn to tell the whole truth, he climbed aboard the witness chair, turned to Judge Horner, and stated in a rich Wanchese brogue, "Judge, all that Chief Whittington said was true, but there ain't no way he could say I was indecently exposed. Sittin' down there in front of the movie house, there just ain't no way he could see my . . . uh, well, Judge, my you-know-what. He was too far away!"

Judge Horner didn't crack a smile as he inquired of the defendant, "Would you rather plead guilty to the charge of improper equipment?"

Delighted, the defendant replied, "Reckon I would, Judge, reckon I would!"

Horner assessed him the costs of court and told the smiling solicitor to call his next case.

How's That?

Soon after the Korean War, a young man from Haywood County sued his wife for divorce, claiming she had given birth to a baby girl eighteen months after he had gone to Korea.

The young lady took the stand and revealed, during cross-examination, that the baby did, indeed, belong to her husband.

"Just a moment," the lawyer for the plaintiff said. "Do I understand you correctly? Are you saying that your husband fathered this baby girl nine months after he went to Korea?"

"Yes, sir."

"How can that be?"

"Sir," she stammered, "he came to me in a dream one night."

"In a dream!" the attorney shouted. "Are you saying you had sexual relations with a ghost?"

"Yes, sir."

At that point, the judge broke into the proceedings.

"I don't believe I have ever heard anything like that before," the judge said, and then directing his attention to the packed courtroom, asked, "Is there anyone in this courtroom who ever had sexual relations with a ghost?"

A farmer in bibbed overalls, seated on the back bench, slowly, reluctantly, raised his hand. For a moment, the surprised judge stared at the farmer, and then said, "Sir, will you please approach the bench?"

The farmer walked slowly to the bench. He cupped his hand to his ear to better hear what the judge asked.

"Sir, do you mean to tell me that you have had sexual relations with a ghost?"

"GHOST!" the old man said. "Oh, no, Your Honor—I thought you said GOAT!"

Fair or Foul?

Uncle George Smathers of Balsam was a venerable man in his eighties who sported a long, white beard and looked every inch the mountain man.

He was an old man in the days when everyone in the county came to town on Saturday to stand on the street, swap knives, tell lies, and spit tobacco juice all over the curb. In Sylva, where Uncle George came every Saturday, the favorite loafing spot was a long concrete stoop that ran the length of the front of the Sylva Supply Store.

It was on that stoop one Saturday that Uncle George noticed a young man of his acquaintance sitting a few feet away with his head hanging down between his knees and a woebegone expression on his face.

Uncle George moved over beside the young fellow and asked, "Son, this ain't like you. Why are you lookin' so glum and sad?"

"You'd look glum and sad, too," the young man said, "if you was coming up in court next week before John M. Queen for rape."

"Rape!" Uncle George exclaimed. The old man thought a few moments, then turned to the younger man and asked, "Was this rape supposed to have happened July seventh last?"

The younger man peered inquiringly at the older. "Yes, it was," he said.

"Was it supposed to have been with that new girl up the creek?"

"Yeah, that's the one."

"And was it supposed to have happened at the spring head on North Fork Creek?"

"That's the place!" The young man was sitting bolt

upright by then. "How'd you know that, Uncle George?"

"Because, by gum," Uncle George said, "I seed it happen."

The young man stared incredulously.

"Every afternoon," the old man said, "I take a long walk. That day I walked up to the spring head and sat down on a log about thirty feet above it. I seed you and that gal come up there hand in hand, seed you lay down on the moss, and I seed ever'thing that went on."

"Oh, Lordy!" The boy jumped up. "Would you be a witness for me in court?"

"Well, I ain't one that likes to hang around the courts," Uncle George said, "but I reckon I'll be there Monday morning."

And so on the Monday following when Solicitor John M. Queen called the case and admonished all squeamish women to leave the courtroom because he was going to "call a spade a spade," the state put up its evidence.

The girl testified how the young man had dragged her off the trail, tore her clothing off, and how he had raped and ravished her. She pointed out the defendant, at Queen's urging, and said, "That's him, all right—that's him sittin' right there."

Queen looked mildly surprised, after he had rested the state's case, when the defense called Uncle George Smathers to the stand.

"State your name, please," the defendant's lawyer told Uncle George.

"George Smathers."

"How old are you, Mr. Smathers?"

"If I live till October fourteenth next," Uncle George said, "I'll be eighty-nine."

"Where were you on the afternoon of July seventh last, Mr. Smathers?"

"I was settin' on a log about thirty feet above a spring head on North Fork."

"I see. Well, did you see the defendant and the prosecuting witness that afternoon?"

"I shore did."

"Did you see them walk up to the spring head and lie down in the moss?"

"I shore did."

"Did you see everything that went on?"

"I shore did. Couldn't take my eyes off'n 'em!"

"Well, from what you saw and from what you heard, would you call what you saw rape?"

Before John Queen had time to object, Uncle George stood up in the witness box and blurted, "Lord, no, I didn't see no rape. That was the fairest matin' I ever seen!"

His testimony won the case for his young friend.

The Other One

Joshua was a recurrent defendant often charged with the manufacture of bootleg whiskey in Columbus County Superior Court.

After a particularly arduous and boring day of court, Judge Raymond Mallard, who later became chief judge of the North Carolina Court of Appeals, relaxed somewhat and asked of Joshua as he passed by, "Joshua, do you reckon you're related to the Joshua of the Old Testament who made the sun stand still?"

"Naw, suh," Joshua replied very solemnly, "I's the Joshua what made the moon shine."

His Own Justice

In the days of old Wake Forest, there was a recorder's court judge who sometimes believed in making up his own law as he went along.

A carnival came to town and set up on the outskirts of the campus, and the young, new town police officer arrested the hoochie-coochie dancer and charged that her actions were bad for the morals of the students.

At the conclusion of the officer's testimony, the judge was still undecided about the verdict, so he ordered the young woman to perform her dance for him in the courtroom.

For the next ten minutes she wiggled out of most of her clothing, making the judge's eyeballs pop.

When she finished dancing, the judge slammed down his gavel. "Not guilty," he yelled. "Next case."

"But, Judge," said the young officer, rushing to the bench, "aren't you even going to fine her?"

"Yes, sir, sonny," said the judge, "just as soon as the sun goes down."

His Just Dues

The young man, obviously a hick, came before the court as plaintiff in a suit involving another man who had smashed into the plaintiff's shiny new automobile and smashed it to bits.

"So, now," said the judge, "you are here to sue him for damages, eh?"

"Heck no, Judge," said the hick. "I already got plenty of damages. What I'm suing him for is some repairs."

2 • *Have Gavel, Will Travel*

When people think of a judge, the classic stereotype of the prim, proper, and stern black-robed grandfather usually comes to mind. This picture isn't always true. In fact, it's more often not true. Here is a collection of legends and stories told by judges themselves—stories about themselves or other judges. A certain very human flavor emerges along with the prim and proper. You be the judge!

Judge B. T. "Buzz" Falls, Jr.

One of the most colorful superior court judges who ever held court in the Thirtieth Judicial District was B. T. Falls, Jr., who was affectionately known as "Buzz." He had a way of relieving tension for those of us who worked in his courts.

One afternoon in Graham County, where Buzz and I were holding court, I had arraigned and tried a man for murder. It had been an exceptionally hard case, and just before I was to argue the case to the jury, the judge motioned for me to approach the bench.

He whispered, "See that woman on the front row of the jury?"

I knew the one he was talking about. She was about five feet, two inches tall, and must have weighed three hundred and fifty pounds.

"If I told her to 'haul ass,' " Buzz said, "she'd have to make two trips!"

Judge Falls was in Jackson County for a superior court session, and the sheriff assigned a young deputy named "Frog" Lewis as the courtroom bailiff. For some reason, Frog had developed a terrible fear of Judge Falls. On occasion, just to liven things up, I exploited that fear.

We were in the midst of a trial of a defendant for safecracking, and I had the safe in question, which weighed six thousand pounds, hauled up to the court-room to be used for evidence.

The court was at ease for a few minutes, Judge Falls sitting quietly on the bench, while I explained to the new bailiff the procedures I would use.

"Now, Frog," I said, "I will say, 'The State offers into evidence what has been identified as State's Exhibit A, to wit a safe,' and I will request that the bailiff hand the same up to the jury."

"Buck," Frog said, looking at the safe, "I don't think I can do it," and then he cast a glance at the judge, "but if *he* says to do it, I will."

Judge Falls believes there is no place for uncertainty or indecisiveness on the bench. To illustrate this belief, he tells a story about the most indecisive judge he knows, a man who was said to be so indecisive that when he went into a men's room he wet his pants trying to decide which urinal to use.

Once, the indecisive judge was presented with an order by an attorney to have a child legitimated. The judge examined the order and said to the attorney, "I'm afraid you will have to add this and this and this before I can sign this order."

The attorney took his order back to the clerk of court and made the suggested changes. But upon receiving the revised order for signature, the judge read it over again and said, "I'm afraid that you are going to have to take it back to the clerk's office and add two other things, which are . . . ." He pointed out the additions.

Again the attorney went to the clerk, and once again returning the order to the judge, heard him intone, "Well, I really don't think it is completely right, but I am going to sign it with the understanding that some day in the future this order might be before another judge who might disagree with me and declare your infant a 'technical bastard'."

"That's strange, Judge," said the attorney, "because the last time I took this order to the clerk, that's what he called you!"

Judge Falls was one of the powers of North Carolina jurisprudence. I knew him first as a state legislator, then as a solicitor, and finally as a superior court judge, an office he held when he died. He was stern but fair, and totally impartial with litigants. He was tough on punishment: If he wanted a defendant to serve five years he gave him twenty, because he knew the parole commission would release him after one-fourth of his sentence.

Holding court with Judge Falls in Graham County, I

had a case in which the defendant was charged with breaking and entering, and larceny. The case was wholly circumstantial; we had no eyeball witnesses, no codefendant to testify, and no admission of guilt by the defendant.

At the close of the evidence and the arguments of counsel for the defense and myself, Buzz took a recess and called me into his chambers.

"Buck," he said, "you know I've got to define 'circumstantial evidence' to the jury. The United States Supreme Court has stated what the definition is, but it takes two printed pages to define it, and I can't understand it that way, so I know this jury can't. I'm going to have to tell 'em what it means in plain English."

We returned to the courtroom, and the judge turned to the jury. "Now, members of the jury," he said, "it is necessary that I define what is meant by the term 'circumstantial evidence.' If I used the definition given by the supreme court, nobody in this courtroom would know what I'm talking about, so I'm going to tell it to you plain.

"If tomorrow morning you back out of your carport and the concrete is clean as a whistle, and tomorrow afternoon you come home from work and there, right in the middle of your carport, is a pile of cow manure, members of the jury, that's damned good circumstantial evidence that there's been a cow in your carport."

The jury understood. The twelve retired to deliberate for about long enough to smoke a cigarette, and came back with a verdict of guilty.

If Buzz Falls didn't like you, he found a way to let you know. He had little liking for the sheriff of a certain county a few years ago, and as they were of different political persuasion, the judge's dislike was intensified.

In the county seat, the courthouse stood in the middle of the town square, and in order to traverse Main Street you had to drive around the courthouse on a one-way street with cars parked on both sides and room for only one car to pass through. That one-way street was the only one on which you could pass through town.

I drove Judge Falls to town one morning to hold court, and when we drove around the courthouse at nine o'clock, there was no parking place reserved for the judge.

As we circled the courthouse the second time, the judge said, "Buck, stop the car right here. Take your keys and lock the doors." I did as instructed, blocking the town's through traffic. We went into the courthouse and to the second-floor courtroom.

In fifteen minutes, the noise of honking automobile horns outside was so loud we couldn't hear anything else. I looked out the window, and cars were backed up three-quarters of a mile to the bypass. All the drivers were angry and blowing their horns, and the din was deafening. I went to the bench and told the judge, as loud as I could holler, that the clerk of court said he would take my keys and find a parking place.

The judge replied, "Buck, that's not the clerk's job. The sheriff is the one who's supposed to reserve the judge a parking place. Send for that weak-minded bastard, give *him* the keys, and tell him that tomorrow morning when we get here, there had better be a parking place."

Next morning, when we arrived, there were three spaces reserved, with a deputy standing guard over each.

In his younger days, when he was a practicing attorney, Buzz Falls said he defended a man on a charge of crime against nature, specifically for having had intercourse with a female pony.

A neighbor who had been standing at his back door testified that he had seen the defendant walk out his back door, down to the pasture fence, across the fence, and up to the pony.

The jurors, all male, and mostly farmers wearing bibbed overalls, were to a man chewing tobacco. Each had a brass spittoon before him. On the front row of the jury box was a corpulent farmer, leaning forward, soaking in every word, unable to spit for fear he would miss something.

Just as the witness testified that the defendant walked up to the pony and with his left hand grasping the pony's tail and his right unbuttoning his "overhauls," the witness turned to the judge and asked, "Do I have to tell the rest, Your Honor?"

"Yes," said the judge, "you have to tell everything you saw."

"Well," said the witness, "that pony shit all over him."

With that, the juror on the front row cut loose and spat a quart into his spittoon, and jabbing the juror to his left with his elbow, remarked in a voice heard throughout the courtroom, "They'll do it ever' time!"

Once again in Jackson County, Frog Lewis was assigned as bailiff during one of Judge Falls's terms, and knowing of Frog's fear of the judge, who was really a gentle man under that frightening facade, I pulled a spur-of-the-moment trick on Frog.

My office in the Jackson County courthouse was at the end of the hall, looking out into the foyer, and on the left off the foyer was the judge's chambers.

During a recess, I took Frog into my office, left the door open, and when I heard the judge coming along, I said, loud enough for him to hear, "Frog, you're gonna have to stop calling Judge Falls a son of a bitch. He's going to hear you one of these times."

Frog saw the judge just outside the door. He paled as white as a sheet.

"God-a-mighty, Buck," he exclaimed, "there he comes. I think he heard you!"

Frog absolutely refused to return to the courtroom that afternoon, and the sheriff had to send over another deputy.

Judge Falls treated everyone alike in his court: He was even-handed enough that he invariably gave everyone some active time, and his sense of humor was such that few of the defendants could take exception to his remarks.

He once took a guilty plea in Jackson County from a man of color who had cut another to the extent that more than four hundred stitches were required to sew up the injured man.

Before sentencing, the judge asked the defendant, "Why did you cut this man so many times?"

"Your Honor," the defendant replied, "he called me a black son of a bitch."

"Oh, I see," said the judge, "recognized you, did he?"

Buzz once had to sentence a confirmed criminal of about sixty years of age on a charge that carried a sixty-year sentence. The man had spent two-thirds of his life in jail already, and apparently was unable to stay out of trouble.

Buzz sentenced him to the full sixty years, figuring that was the last time any judge would have to deal with him.

"Judge," remarked the man, "I don't think I can build that much time, not at my age."

"Well, just do the best you can," the judge replied.

As the sheriff led the man from the courtroom, he looked back at Buzz and said, "I hope you die and go to hell, you old son of a bitch."

The sheriff stopped and held the man, waiting to see what Buzz wanted to do about the outburst.

"Take him on, Sheriff," Buzz said. "I'm not going to hold him in contempt. I guess he really meant it."

Judge Falls has always had a penchant for saying what was on his mind, whether at home or in court. He presided over a murder case in Haywood County a few years ago. When all evidence had been submitted, the defense attorneys had argued for the defendant, and I had argued against him, Judge Falls sent the jury to the jury room to deliberate a verdict.

The jury had been sequestered from the time of its selection and was staying at a motel owned by John Queen, son of the late Solicitor John M. Queen.

Deliberation started about five o'clock on a Wednesday afternoon, and Judge Falls allowed the jury two hours before the members were sent to dinner and taken to the motor court for the night.

At nine-thirty the next morning, deliberations began again, with all jurors pacified by a hearty breakfast. At twelve-thirty Judge Falls allowed the jury until two o'clock for lunch. At three o'clock he called the jury into the courtroom to ask if the members were making any progress. The foreman reported that the jury was divided eleven to one, and the judge, thinking much progress had been made, sent the jury back to deliberate further.

At five-thirty the courtroom was in a lull, and Judge Falls brought the jury back and asked the foreman how the proceedings were going.

"Your Honor," the foreman reported, "we are still deadlocked at eleven to one."

The judge turned to the bailiff. "Mr. Bailiff," he asked, "where are you taking these jury members for their meals?"

"I'm taking them to the Steak House, Your Honor," the bailiff replied.

"All right, Mr. Bailiff," Judge Falls said, "just don't take the jurors out tonight. Let them stay and deliberate while you go to the Steak House and bring back eleven good T-bone steaks and one bale of hay for their dinner."

The distinguished attorney, Senator Roy Francis, once represented a defendant who was charged in five cases of felony larceny. The case came before Judge Falls in Haywood County Superior Court.

I had called one of the cases for trial and had presented the state's evidence. I rested the state's case, and it was time for the defendant to present evidence, if he desired.

Judge Falls asked Senator Francis if he had any evidence for the defendant.

The senator responded, "Your Honor, the defendant desires to take the stand."

"Well, go ahead and call him," said the judge in a strong voice. "He might as well take the stand; he appears to have already taken everything else in the county."

Judge William Z. Wood

In 1976, during a superior court session in Haywood County, with Judge William Z. Wood of Winston-Salem presiding, most of the cases were from an extensive under-cover operation involving the sale of controlled substances —drugs—in the county.

Realizing that the prisons of North Carolina were loaded to the gills and bursting at the seams, Judge Wood took the position that except for repeaters he would put the defendants on stiff probation and impose rather substantial fines.

The fines he imposed that session amounted to more than $200,000, all of which went to the public school fund of Haywood County. At the conclusion of the session, an editorial appeared in *The Waynesville Mountaineer* regarding the large amount of money that would enable the schools to do many things they would not have been able to do with the limited tax funds available.

The editorial concluded that "Judge William Z. Wood is the best thing that has happened to Haywood County since the WPA!"

Over the years, Judge Wood and I have almost developed a brother relationship between us. He was raised on a little mountain farm near Dobson in Surry County, and like a lot of others, grew up "poor as a church mouse." He pulled himself up by his bootstraps to become the senior resident superior court judge of Forsyth County.

For years he has sworn to the truth of his favorite story, to wit:

A mule is a peculiar critter. If you've ever observed one, you know that it won't go under anything where his "years will tetch."

When Bill was a youngster, his pappy's mule was not endowed with the usual length of ears of even an ordinary mule. His, in fact, were about as short as the ears of a horse.

Bill said Pappy built a small log building out back to house their mule in inclement weather. He had measured the door to just admit his mule without his ears touching a twenty-four-inch oak log across the top of the door. The floor of the stall was dirt, but Pap always said he wasn't going to floor that shed for a damned mule when he hadn't even floored all of his own house.

One morning he went out to get his mule for Bill to commence plowing, and bless the Lord!—there lay his mule, dead as a doorknob. After a day's burying, he struck out to hunt another mule. He found a beautiful bay mule at the local animal sale and proceeded to buy it, not realizing that it was the longest-eared mule in the county.

Arriving home, he took his new mule to the mule shed and undertook to lead him in, but when that critter started in the door, "his years tetched" that big oak log framing the top of the door and wouldn't go a step farther. All the beating, hollering, and cussing, wouldn't budge him.

Knowing the propensities of this animal, Pap went to the tool shed, got a chisel and a maul, and commenced chiseling away on that well-seasoned oak over the doorway.

The sun beamed down, the temperature rose, and the old man was approaching a heat stroke when his wife walked out and saw what he was doing.

"Pap," she said, "how come you're getting yourself all het up chiseling that log on top? Wouldn't it be easier to take a shovel and dig some dirt out at the bottom of the door?"

Pap snorted. "Hell's fire, woman," he snapped, "didn't you hear me say hit was his years that was too long, not his legs?"

Out in the deep woods beyond Judge Wood's boyhood home near Winston-Salem, a man named John Henry and a woman named Maybelle had gone together steadily for more than ten years without serious mention of matrimony.

One beautiful summer evening they were parked in a secluded area in such an amorous mood that Maybelle's fragrance simply overcame John Henry, and he popped the question.

Maybelle was delighted. "I thought you was never gonna ax me," she said, "and my answer is yes."

"Hot dog!" John Henry yelled.

"However," Maybelle continued, "there is one condition. If I marry you, you will have to give me a wedding exactly like the biggest wedding ever held in Winston-Salem."

"Shucks," said John Henry, "that ain't no problem. I got plenty o' money up there in the top of the Wachovie building. You just go down to *The Winston-Salem Journal*, look through them papers, and pick out the wedding you want, and I'll give it to you exactly, persactly like you wants it."

So down to the paper office went Maybelle, who looked through the papers till her eyes hurt. Finally she found the wedding she was looking for—that of R. J. Reynolds, Jr. Its account covered the better part of three pages and described everything in detail except the honeymoon.

Maybelle gave the clipping to John Henry who promptly took it to a florist and told him he wanted a wedding exactly, persactly like that one. Came the wedding day and the florist had really done his work. Inside, the church was bedecked with banks of rare orchids and long-stemmed roses. Fragrant flower petals were scattered on the carpet.

At the appointed hour, John Henry and Maybelle

arrived in a Rolls Royce, entered the crowded church, and went through the motions of a wedding required by law, and then some.

Just before the minister, in his newly-acquired robe trimmed with sable, pronounced them man and wife, a skinny little man burst through the main doors of the church and ran up and down the aisles, pinching all the women on their bosoms. When he pinched the last woman, he ran out the side door and disappeared.

The astonished minister recovered his composure and quickly finished the ceremony. The bride and groom drove off in their Rolls Royce.

Down the road, John Henry turned to Maybelle. "Wasn't that weddin' exactly, persactly like the weddin' I promised you, or was it?"

"Yes, John Henry," smiled Maybelle, "it was everything I wanted." Then a frown replaced the smile, and she asked, "There was one little thing I didn't understand. How come that skinny little fellow run in the church and pinched all the women on their bosoms?"

John Henry withdrew the clipping of the Reynolds' wedding from his pocket, ran his finger down it to the bottom, and said, "Looky here, Maybelle. It says here that as the minister pronounced them husband and wife a nervous little titter ran through the congregation."

Judge Hoyle Sink

Several years ago Hoyle Sink was known by defendants and lawyers alike as "the hanging judge." He had a tendency to throw the book at almost everyone.

Court was in Bryson City and the hanging judge was

presiding. Thad Bryson was solicitor, and I had been employed by the mother of an eighteen-year-old Cherokee Indian named Walkingstick, who was charged with drunken driving.

During those days, most of our Indian college students went to an Indian school in Oklahoma, and my client had come home on a quarter break, had a few beers with a bunch of boys, and was arrested and charged.

I took the case for twenty-five dollars. Court opened on Monday, and I talked with Thad about my case, begging and entreating him almost on bended knee to let me plead my client guilty to reckless driving so he wouldn't lose his driver's license.

Knowing the reputation of Judge Sink, but having never been in his court before, Thad told me, "Buck, you see that damned old judge sitting up there? He's mean as hell. He's liable to put us both in jail if I let you do that. Frankly, I'm as scared of him as I am of an old bear dog."

I stayed in court from Monday through Friday and Thad held my case open for me. At noon recess on Friday, Thad, the judge, and I were lunching at Sneed's Restaurant across the street from the courthouse.

I was thinking about my case, and suddenly I said to myself, "You idiot! Here you are at lunch with the judge and court's about over. He can't put you in jail over here, even if he doesn't like what you say . . . ."

So I turned to Judge Sink and said, "Your Honor, I've got an Indian named Walkingstick who is charged with driving drunk. If you take his license he can't go back to Oklahoma to college. I've been trying all week to get the solicitor here to let me plead him to reckless driving."

Judge Sink asked, "Well, what did he say?"

I gulped and answered, "Judge, he said he couldn't let

me do it on account of you. He said he was as scared of you as he was of a bear dog."

At that, the judge almost went under the table laughing, but he said nothing further about the case at the table.

Finished with lunch, the three of us walked back to the courthouse, and as we passed the office of Clerk of Court Henry Truett, Judge Sink said, "You two go on upstairs. I want to stop by the clerk's office for a minute."

Thad and I went on up, he muttering under his breath about what I had said to the judge about his fears, knowing he had Sink with him in the district for the next six months.

Court reopened at two o'clock, and the cases were clicked off till we were down to one—mine.

In his stentorian voice, Thad called out, "Walkingstick!"

The defendant jumped up and headed toward me, but Judge Sink held up his hand and stopped the defendant, turned to Thad, and said, "Mr. Solicitor, my calendar shows you've already disposed of that case."

"No, Your Honor," Thad said. "I haven't even called it till just now."

"Don't dispute my word, Mr. Solicitor," the judge said. "I said you have already disposed of that case. Mr. Sheriff, adjourn this court sine die."

The sheriff did as he was told, the judge left the courtroom and headed back to Greensboro, where he lived, and as soon as he was out of sight, Thad and I hot-footed it down to the clerk's office to see what the score was.

Upon inquiry, the clerk told us that when Judge Sink came in after lunch, he sat down in a chair and convulsed in laughter for a full five minutes, then told the clerk that a laugh like that he hadn't had in fifty years, and that it called not for a plea of reckless driving in my case but for a straight-out dismissal of the charges.

"Please attend to that, Mr. Clerk," he had instructed Truett.

So I got my twenty-five dollars, my client kept his license, Thad eventually recovered from his shock, and Hoyle Sink got the best belly laugh of his career.

Judge Sink loved Scotch whiskey, though I hasten to say it never interfered with his work. Once while I was in the legislature and the semiannual Democratic Jefferson-Jackson Dinner was being held in Raleigh, hotel rooms were nonexistent; they were not even to be had at a premium.

I had a room in the Sir Walter Hotel, where the dinner was held, and after the dinner I walked into the spacious lobby and spied Judge Sink seated in an easy chair, his silver-headed cane resting against a duffle bag at his feet.

I went over and told him who I was, reminding him of what he had done for the Indian student in Bryson City, and asked him where he was staying.

"Buck," he said, "I guess I'm staying right here in this chair. There ain't a room to be had from here to Greensboro."

"You're going to do nothing of the kind," I told him. "Here's the key to Room 747. It's my room. I'll be insulted if you don't take it, because I can bunk with some other representative."

Judge Sink was getting along in years and was relieved at the thought of sleeping in a bed instead of a lounge chair. He accepted my offer, but before he went upstairs, he said to me:

"Buchanan, I'm parked a half a mile from here, and all my Scotch is in my car. Reckon you could scrounge up a bottle for me to take up to the room?"

I told him if that was all he had to worry about, he would live another hundred years. I called the room of my uncle, Harry Buchanan, a lobbyist for the theater industry, told him what I wanted, and he said to come on up.

I went to his room and got three fifths of the finest Scotch, took them to the judge's room, and I feel confident he spent a restful and pleasant night.

Anyway, he has been a friend of mine ever since.

Judge Lacy Thornburg

Superior Court Judge Lacy Thornburg of Sylva was once holding court in Buncombe County when a notorious drunk came before the bar, charged with being in an intoxicated condition, and also with malicious damage to property.

The facts disclosed that the fellow had been picked up in front of the Buncombe County courthouse in a highly inebriated condition. He was placed in a cell in the Buncombe County jail and thirty minutes later was found lying on a bunk with the mattress on fire. The fire was the basis for the malicious-damage-to-property charge.

When the man stepped before the judge, Lacy asked how he pleaded: guilty or not guilty?

He hauled himself erect and said, "Your Honor, I will be glad to plead guilty to being publicly drunk because I was. I was terribly drunk.

"But I am not guilty of the damage-to-property charge," he added, "because I'm pretty sure that bed was already on fire when I got in it!"

Holding a term of superior court in Burke County, Judge Thornburg was presented with a petition filed by a young woman who sought the court's approval to have an abortion.

A mountain man somewhat skeptical of abortions, Lacy always required the petitioner to state to him in her own words some really good and compelling reason why such authority should be granted.

When he asked the petitioner to state precisely why she was requesting an abortion, she thought a moment and replied, "Well, Your Honor, the best reason I have is that after careful consideration and thought, I frankly don't think it's mine!"

Harold Hoffman of Franklin was a court reporter for years. He was as full of bull as the Mississippi is full of water, and was all the time pulling people's legs and telling jokes.

We were holding court in Haywood County with Judge Thornburg on the bench, and the three of us—Lacy, Harold, and I—went to lunch together. When we went up to pay our checks, Harold realized he had run off from home without his wallet. He borrowed five dollars from Lacy, paid his bill, and when we got back to the courthouse he cashed a check at the tax office.

Lacy and I had gone on upstairs to the courtroom which was packed with defendants and spectators. The court was called to order and as soon as the people were seated and things were quiet, Harold walked in to take his seat at his little recording machine.

He detoured up by the bench, however, and with a theatrical gesture, pulled a five-dollar bill from his pocket and, in a voice which could be heard in the rear of the courtroom, said, "Here, Lacy, old buddy, is what I promised you for fixing that ticket for me."

That was the first and last time I ever saw Lacy speechless.

Judge Thornburg was holding court in Charlotte once when he received a report from a grand jury stating that the interior of the Mecklenburg County jail should be painted because of the filthy graffiti on the walls. Lacy promised to send a copy of the report to the county commissioners with directions to take some action.

Later in the day, he found some time and instructed the bailiff to take him upstairs to see the jail.

As they entered a large holding area, perhaps forty by forty feet, where the jailer put prisoners to be later assigned to cells, Lacy glanced up near the top of the wall and there, painted in large black letters with shoe polish, was the following message: "STAY OUT OF THORNBERRY'S COURT. HE WILL FLAT ASS GIVE YOU TIME!"

Judge James H. Pou Bailey

Back in the good old days of twenty or more years ago, Superior Court Judge James H. Pou Bailey of Raleigh flew his own airplane to various assignments around the state. He once flew into Eastern North Carolina to hold a court session in a small county on the coast near the South Carolina border. He had telephoned the sheriff of the county and asked him to meet him at the Wilmington airport and chauffeur him to court.

When the judge climbed into the sheriff's car, the sheriff switched on his blue light and siren and sped out of the airport as if he were on the way to a fire.

"Mr. Sheriff," the judge said, "why have we got the blue light and siren on?"

"Oh, hell, Judge," said the sheriff, "I thought a dead game sport like you might enjoy an exciting ride."

"Well, I don't like it."

The sheriff switched off the light and siren but continued down the road at sixty miles an hour or better.

Soon the judge saw a mileage sign to Shallotte flash by. "Sheriff," he asked, "is Shallotte between Wilmington and your county seat?"

"Oh, no, Judge," the sheriff said, "Shallotte is way up in the western end of the county. It would be way out of our way to go to Shallotte. Besides, we don't have the time this morning, but if you want to go to Shallotte before you leave, why, I'll be glad to drive you there."

About that time another sign flashed by that read: "Shallotte City Limit—Bird Sanctuary." The judge said, "Sheriff, I believe we are already in Shallotte."

The sheriff looked at the surroundings. "By George, Judge," he said, "I believe we are in Shallotte. I must've took the wrong road."

"That must be your problem," said Judge Bailey. "Pull into that filling station and ask the man how to get to the county seat."

"Oh, I know how to get there," said the sheriff.

"Well, pull in and ask him anyway," the judge ordered.

Meekly, the sheriff did as told, and the station operator looked at him as if he were crazy. He told him to go straight down Highway 17. "You can't miss it," he said.

"Thanks," said the red-faced sheriff, and Judge Bailey hoped the sheriff had learned a lesson.

Finally they came to the county seat and then the courthouse and the sheriff took Judge Bailey up the back stairs to the judge's chambers. To Bailey's utter amazement, he observed a desk pulled across the end of the tiny room with a bathroom commode behind it.

"Mr. Sheriff," Judge Bailey exploded, "what the hell is this?"

"Your Honor, this is the judge's chambers."

"To be sure," Judge Bailey said, "it is the best-equipped one in the state. To what do we owe this unusual arrangement?"

"Well, Judge," the sheriff explained, "a few years back we had a lady judge come down here and she raised all grades of hell because there wasn't a can on the second floor and she had to go all the way down to the basement at recess to go to the john. She said she wouldn't hold any court unless we put a can up here on the courtroom floor. So we called a plumber and told him to get hot and put a can in that same day. He said the only place he could put it was in this corner because this is the only place he could tie it in with the plumbing.

"We told him to go ahead, figuring we could build two walls around it, put a door in one of them, and she'd have a little closet, but after he got the commode in and laid out the walls, we realized that there wouldn't be room to open the door with a desk in the room.

"So we said, what the hell—a chair is a chair. She just might as well turn the seat down and sit on that as sit on any other sort of chair, so we pulled the desk up in front of the can and when she wanted to use it for its regular purpose, she could lock the office door. Otherwise, it serves as a good desk chair. Right?"

During that session, Judge Bailey felt like a full-fledged idiot, holding conferences in judge's chambers with dignified attorneys, sitting all the while in his black robe on a commode!

Judge Bailey was assigned to a court session in Lee County one fall, and the weather as he drove to the courthouse was misty, rainy, and nasty.

He approached a man walking toward town on the side of the road. Wearing bibbed overalls, the man didn't try to hitch a ride but continued a fast shuffle toward town.

"That fellow is going to Sanford," the judge told himself. "He's not out here thumbing, begging for a ride, but is walking and making progress. I'm going to give him a lift."

He pulled over, opened the car door, and said, "Brother, are you going to Sanford?"

"Yes, I am."

"Well, get in and I'll take you there."

Driving on toward town, the judge said, "Look, Mister, I am going a little way on the other side of town. I'm going to the courthouse, and I will be glad to drop you anywhere in Sanford that you want to go."

"Matter of fact," the man said, "I'm going to the courthouse, too."

"Oh?" queried the judge. "Do you have a case down there?"

"Yes, I do," the man said, "and I'm right much worried about it. They tell me they have a fat son of a bitch from Raleigh down there that would hang his own grandmother just to see her kick."

By that time, Judge Bailey had figured out that he had asked one question too many. He let the man off in front of the courthouse, drove around behind and parked, and went up the back stairs to his chambers.

At ten o'clock, Judge Bailey told the bailiff to go out and open court. "I'll be right behind you," he said.

When he walked into the courtroom, his passenger looked up and saw who the judge was. He burst from the place where he was standing, ran up the aisle, out the back door, and into the street—and it took two deputies a block and a half to run him down.

The man was charged with assault with a deadly weapon doing serious bodily injury, and had the clearest case of self-defense that Judge Bailey had ever heard.

At the conclusion of the state's evidence, the defendant's lawyer moved for dismissal, and Judge Bailey said, "Granted."

The man leaned over to his lawyer and asked, "What did he say?"

The lawyer said, "Don't bother me now. Get out of here before the damned fool changes his mind."

Like preachers or doctors, attorneys and judges love to tell stories on each other. One of Judge Bailey's favorite stories concerns Judge W. H. S. Burgwyn.

Burgwyn, Bailey said, was holding court in Robeson County where "Big John" Reagan was solicitor. About mid-morning on Monday, Judge Burgwyn called Big John up to the bench and asked, "Mr. Solicitor, what is that nice-looking young lady sitting in the front row of the courtroom doing here? This is no place for a lady."

"Judge," said Big John, "she's a defendant."

"A defendant?" the judge asked.

"She's charged with driving under the influence."

"Well," said Judge Burgwyn, "she's not guilty. I can tell you that right now."

"We've got a right good case against her, Judge."

"We'll see," said the judge, "we'll see."

In due time, John called her case. A highway patrolman testified that he had observed a car weaving in the road, running off the pavement onto the shoulder every now and then. He said he was suspicious that the driver was under the influence of alcohol, so he stopped the car with his blue light and a tap on the siren.

The officer said he walked up to the window of the car and detected a strong odor of alcohol. He asked the defendant, who was driving the car, to step out, and as she did, he said, she stumbled. He asked for her driver's license and she fumbled in her purse and passed it twice before she recognized it. He asked her to follow him back to the patrol car and she staggered as she walked along the shoulder of the road, and he said she seemed to be very nervous and upset. In his opinion, he said, she was under the influence of some alcoholic beverage.

The defendant denied the charge, but very passively.

When Judge Burgwyn's time came to charge the jury, he said, "Now, ladies and gentlemen of the jury, in this case the State of North Carolina has offered evidence which in substance tends to show that the highway patrolman observed this lady driving a car, that it was weaving in the road and occasionally ran off the shoulder.

"Now, ladies and gentlemen, everybody knows how women drive.

"The officer testified," the judge said, "that he turned on his blue light and she stopped, and he went up alongside the car and detected an odor of alcohol. Everybody knows that women use a lot of perfume and perfume has an alcohol base. It is no small wonder that he smelled alcohol when he got alongside the car.

"He said as she stepped out of the car, she stumbled. I

will address that in a moment. He said she fumbled in her purse for her driver's license. All of you men on the jury know what your wife's pocketbook looks like. If she could find a grand piano in under five minutes it would be a miracle. You ladies on the jury: Look in your pocketbooks right now and pull out your driver's licenses. Let's see how long it takes you.

"The officer said the young lady was nervous. It would be remarkable if she was not nervous—a young girl driving on the road at night, stopped by a strange man with a blue light and siren. Anyone would be nervous.

"He said she staggered as she walked down the shoulder of the road. Ladies and gentlemen of the jury, the shoulders of these roads are rough; they are not meant for walking. Look at the heels this young woman is wearing: four inches high. It is a miracle that she didn't fall and skin her pretty knees.

"That, ladies and gentlemen," he concluded, "is what the state's evidence tends to show. What it really shows, if it shows anything at all, is for you to say."

In about five minutes the jury returned a verdict of *"Not Guilty!"*

Judge Burgwyn leaned over the bench and looked Big John Reagan right in the eye, and said, "Mr. Solicitor, I told you so!"

Judge Hal Hammer Walker

Back in the days when "court week" was even bigger than the Fourth of July, Judge Hal Hammer Walker of Asheboro, resident superior court judge of Judicial District 19-B, held a session of court in Carteret County.

"I remember it was Friday," Judge Walker recalled, "and it was hotter than the hinges of hell in that old courtroom. The only ventilation system was a surplus Pratt and Whitney aircraft engine which made so much noise it could not be run, and I wanted to get through with that case so I could enjoy some fishing with my good friend, Claud Wheatly."

The case, which had begun on Monday morning, involved the Torrens Act. Judge Walker had not heard of the Torrens Act since law school and didn't remember what he had learned, if anything, about it then, but he told those involved that he would make a stab at it.

Former Judge Tom Smith-Jones was in the case, as was Claud Wheatly, and in order to expedite matters, Judge Walker asked the jury to come in at nine o'clock on Friday morning and argument would start immediately thereafter.

The jury showed up on schedule, the courtroom audience was seated, Claud Wheatly was there, but Judge Smith-Jones was nowhere in sight.

Judge Walker called the bailiff to the bench. "Do you know where Judge Smith-Jones is?" Judge Walker asked.

"Judge, I don't know," the bailiff answered, "but I'll go look for him."

Judge Walker called Wheatly to the bench and asked him to go look for the judge also.

In a few minutes, Wheatly returned to the courtroom, apparently having a hard time keeping a straight face. He approached the bench and whispered, "Judge, don't make any comment; just follow me."

Wheatly led Judge Walker into the lawyers' conference room, and there stood Judge Smith-Jones, a huge man, with his large expanse of belly and other parts of his body exposed to the sun at one of the windows.

When he turned around, Judge Walker had trouble controlling himself. "Judge," he said, "I don't know of any delicate way of asking a man how he managed to wet all over himself, but how did you?"

Judge Smith-Jones sort of chuckled. "I went into the judge's chambers," he said, "to use the only facilities on this floor, and I guess I was concentrating so much on what I was going to say to the jury, that when I zipped down I didn't realize that I had got hold of a frazzle of shirttail by mistake!"

Judge Walker was making some effort to be helpful, but got little help from others present. Wheatly suggested that since Judge Smith-Jones was a Mason, perhaps he might wear his Masonic apron into court to cover up the damage.

Judge Walker suggested they send the bailiff to the judge's home and get a new pair of pants, but Smith-Jones informed him that he lived too many miles away. "Besides," Smith-Jones said, "I think my breeches will dry off sufficiently in a few minutes."

"Well, we're going to have to proceed pretty soon," Judge Walker said. "There is a tall chair that the bailiff sits in sometimes. If you wish, you may stand behind it and argue the case while the bailiff goes after your fresh pants."

Judge Smith-Jones said he thought that would be a good idea, and in that manner, hiding behind a chair, he began his closing argument to the jury. But the more he got into it, the more heated he became, and soon, without realizing it, he began walking with the chair, back and forth, in front of the jury, and as he made each turn it was obvious to everyone what had happened to him: His light blue pants were rapidly changing to a rather sickly yellow!

When Smith-Jones realized with some embarrassment

that he had given his secret away, he stopped his argument and attempted to apologize to the jury, which, of course, made matters worse.

He told the jury that when a man of his age and girth went to the bathroom he had to be most careful and not get a frazzle of shirttail, and that he apologized to the jury members for holding them up and for dancing back and forth before them.

By then the jury was almost rolling in the aisle.

"Following that," said Judge Walker, "to the best of my ability, I instructed the jury on the Torrens Act, involving a whole island just off the coastal waterway—but it really didn't matter much what I said. There was no way the Torrens Act could follow the Smith-Jones Act that day. Every few seconds, during my instructions, one of the jurors would burst out laughing.

"I have forgotten who won the case, but I have not forgotten that that was the hardest day I have ever spent in court, trying to maintain some degree of judicial propriety and just about failing completely."

There must be a moral in this story told by Judge Walker:

A man had an exceptionally fine hunting dog which bore the name "Lawyer." He rented the dog out on occasion to hunters who had no hounds, and Lawyer worked magnificently.

Those who rented him thought so highly of the dog that they talked his owner into renaming him "Judge." A dog of that intelligence, they reasoned, ought to be placed on a higher pedestal.

A few weeks after renaming the dog, the owner went to

the men who had done the renaming and demanded compensation.

"Compensation for what?" they asked.

"Lawyer was the best hunting dog in the country," the man explained, "until you changed his name to Judge. Now all he wants to do is sit on his ass and growl!"

Sitting on the bench in Winston-Salem, Judge Walker imposed a sentence of not less than five years nor more than seven years on a defendant, and as the convicted man was being led from the courtroom past the bench, he said in a loud voice, "You gray-headed old son of a bitch!"

The bailiff grabbed the prisoner and turned to the bench.

"Judge, did you hear him?"

"Of course, I heard him," Judge Walker said. "Everybody in the courtroom heard him. But take him on out, Sheriff. If someone had just laid five-to-seven on me, an additional thirty days wouldn't bother me a damn bit!

"However," Judge Walker added, "I did resent him calling me gray-headed."

Judge John R. Friday

The first time Judge John R. Friday of Lincolnton held court in Bryson City, he was horrified at some of the facilities in the ancient Swain County courthouse which was used until 1982 when a new and efficient county building was erected. The original building was constructed around the turn of the century, and being thus antiquated, its facilities were extremely poor.

The jury room, just off the courtroom, caught Judge

Friday's attention. It had no doorknob; when the jury went in to deliberate, the door was cracked open about two inches and people in the courtroom could hear all that was said in the jury room.

At the noon recess on his first day in court, Judge Friday entered the jury room and stood astounded by what he saw. There was nothing in the room except a six-foot by four-foot table in the center of the floor, no chairs for the jurors, and in the corner of the room in full view of all was a bathroom commode. There was no enclosure around it.

Judge Friday rounded up a couple of deputy sheriffs and sent them in search of the county commissioners, ordering the commissioners to report to him at two o'clock, the end of the lunch recess.

In his sternest voice, the judge told the commissioners that he would adjourn court until the following morning, and at that time, when court convened, he expected the door of the jury room to be fixed with a knob and lock, and the commode to be enclosed with a partition that would conceal it from view of the other jurors.

The next morning, there was a knob on the door and the door would close. There was also a partition built around the commode—all of four feet high! As the judge had ordered, the partition screened the commode from view of the other jurors, but it still gave no privacy at all.

Judge George Patton

George Patton of Franklin was one of the most remarkable men ever bred in Western North Carolina. When he was a young child, living on a farm, he lost his right arm in a hay baler. His family, realizing he could no longer grow up to work on the farm, arranged for him to get a formal education.

He was graduated from law school, became a member of the state legislature, attorney general of North Carolina for two terms, and resident superior court judge of my district for ten years. He had a native wit unequaled by anyone I have known. Brilliant but homespun, he never let you know what was coming next.

In 1950 when I had been practicing law for about a year, Judge Patton presided at our regular session of superior court in Jackson County.

Just before the noon recess one morning, I was seated inside the bar of the courtroom when a deputy came running and told the sheriff that someone had just been killed in Tannery Flats.

Sheriff Griffin Middleton promptly responded and found a man named Henry standing over the body of the deceased, pistol in hand. There was a tell-tale hole through the dead man's heart. Underneath the deceased, Griff found a large and very sharp butcher knife which Henry insisted the man had been holding in a threatening manner as he advanced on him. Henry, who said he carried the pistol in his pocket in case he saw a snake, maintained that he had shot in self-defense.

The sheriff charged Henry with murder and locked him in jail.

Knowing that the defendant could not make bond and would have to be kept in jail for five months until our next session in October, Judge Patton called me to the bench and told me to go to the jail and talk with Henry about going ahead and pleading guilty to murder in the second degree and start serving his time.

I dutifully talked it over with Henry, but he declined the

judge's offer.

I reported back to the judge, who furrowed his brow, and said, "Buck, go back and tell him to plead guilty to voluntary manslaughter (which carried up to twenty years) and I'll take care of him!"

I hastened to the jail and confronted Henry again. "Henry," I said, "Judge Patton told me if you would plead guilty to voluntary manslaughter, he'd take care of you. You'd better not fail to take advantage of him while he's in that good a humor."

Henry agreed, and I took him before the judge, to whom he entered his plea of guilty to voluntary man-slaughter. The judge drew himself up to his full height and sentenced Henry to prison *for not less than nineteen nor more than twenty years.*

I ran to the bench, leaned over, and said to Judge Patton, "Judge, you said you'd take care of my man if he would plead guilty."

Leaning over the bench, Patton said, "Well, I did, didn't I?"

During that same term of court, as most lawyers customarily did, I invited Judge Patton to my house for lunch. I had a four-year-old son, Mark, who was at the most inquisitive age, and as the judge and I walked into the house, I realized I hadn't told Mark about the judge having only one arm. He kept his empty sleeve pinned up.

Sure enough, as soon as Mark saw the empty sleeve, he peered at it and said, "Say, you ain't got but one arm, have you?"

Quick as a flash, and with that wry smile, Judge Patton held up his empty sleeve, and said, "Well, darned if I ain't!"

Judge Harry C. Martin

Superior Court Judge Harry C. Martin of Asheville, now a member of the North Carolina Court of Appeals, and I once held a session of criminal court in Hayesville, the seat of Clay County, the smallest county in population of the seven counties in the Thirtieth Judicial District.

Hayesville consists of one city block, with the courthouse situated in the center and some stores across the street.

Since there was no motel in Hayesville and the only place to stay was at Walter Moore's boardinghouse on Lake Chatuge, about seven miles from town, that's where Judge Martin and I stayed when we came over on Sunday afternoon to open court on Monday morning.

When we finished court Monday afternoon, the judge and I got in my little diesel Mercedes and started back to Walter Moore's. We drove several times around the block, trying to decide which of the roads led to Highway 64 and thence to the Moore house. Rain was coming down in torrents that day, making it hard for us, strangers in town, to recognize landmarks.

"Judge," I said, "I believe I'll pull into this filling station and ask how to get out of town."

"Go ahead, Buck," Judge Martin said, "but I'm going to scrooch down on the floor where they can't see me. I don't want it to be said that a superior court judge got lost in Hayesville."

The understanding and compassion of the men who sit on the benches in our courts of justice know no ends.

Soon after I became solicitor in 1967, I held a criminal session of court in Jackson County and had a young man, whose name shall remain anonymous, come before the bar of justice, charged with breaking and entering into a cafeteria at Western Carolina University, where he was a student, and taking foodstuffs. The young man was from a large and poor family and testified that he took only what food he needed for his sustenance.

When apprehended, however, he was charged with the felony of breaking and entering into the cafeteria and the felony of larceny. He had been caught red-handed and had no defense, so he came into court and entered pleas of guilty to both felony charges. Judge Martin deferred sentencing until the following day.

Then as now, a plea of guilty to a felony not only had the potential of a prison sentence, but also took the citizenship of the individual, preventing him from voting and from holding public office. On all future applications for employment he would have been required to acknowledge the fact that he was a convicted felon. His life therefore could have been effectively ruined.

He was a senior at Western Carolina, a brilliant young man with what promised to be a bright future.

That afternoon, Judge Martin called me to his chambers, and said, "Buck, you know, I like the impression that young man makes. I like his appearance. I like his demeanor. And he seems to feel really sorry for what he has done.

"I believe this was a one-time thing with him, and if it would not offend your conscience I would like to strike his plea of guilty to the felonies and let him plead no contest to two misdemeanor counts, then put him under a suspended sentence for two years."

I had no objections. I rather liked his idea of judgment in this case.

So on the following day, Judge Martin struck his pleas of guilty to the felonies and let the young man enter pleas to misdemeanors, placed him under a suspended sentence, fined him, and let him go back to school.

The man finished school and returned to his home county. I have kept up with him over the years, and he has been an outstanding citizen. He now holds a high public office and is esteemed by everyone who knows him.

I will always be grateful for the understanding and compassionate attitude taken in this case by Judge Martin. To me, his actions were the epitome of justice at work.

Judge Fred Hasty

Judge Fred Hasty of Charlotte had been in my district for only a short time when we held a criminal session of superior court in Cherokee County. The judge brought his wife along to enjoy the winter beauty of the mountains, and we all met at a motor court in Murphy where officials of the court usually checked in on Sunday afternoon before opening a term of court on Monday.

Judge and Mrs. Hasty had a large corner room, and I had a room next to theirs. I parked my diesel Mercedes in front of my room and retired early.

That night, the temperature dropped into the teens.

I was then and am now an early riser. That morning I arose about four, showered and dressed, and noting how cold it was, I knew I would have difficulty getting the Mercedes to function.

I went out and cranked it up and let it run for about ten minutes, warming up. I noted, when I returned to the room, that in the morning cold the car's engine was extremely loud.

I thought no more of it, and drove to a restaurant that opened early, had breakfast, then went on to the courthouse to get a jump on the day's work.

About nine o'clock, Judge Hasty entered the courthouse and went directly to his chambers. I walked in to inquire how he had slept, and noticed that he was red-eyed.

"Judge Hasty," I said, "did you not sleep well?"

"I slept fine," he snapped, "until sometime in the night when some fool parked a diesel truck in front of my room and left the engine running. It woke both of us and we couldn't go back to sleep. If it happens again," he said, "I'm going to report it to the management."

For the remainder of the time we held that session of court in Murphy, I parked the Mercedes at the far end of the motel lot.

I don't know if Judge Hasty knew it was my Mercedes which kept him awake. If he found out, it was from someone else; I didn't tell him. Whether he knew it or not, he paid me back, possibly inadvertently, later in the week.

He is an avid golfer who plays golf at every opportunity. He is no Nicklaus. He can't slay the ball from the tee. He just pecks it down the fairway. His shots are short but extremely accurate. Each one goes exactly where he wants it to go.

A couple of nights after the Mercedes incident, I was awakened before midnight by a series of sharp thuds, as though someone were throwing stones against a motel door.

I got up, opened my door, and ascertained that the thuds were coming from the vicinity of Judge and Mrs. Hasty's room. Timidly I knocked on the door that connected our rooms.

In his pajamas, Judge Hasty opened the door and invited me in. He had eight or ten golf balls lined up on the carpet and with a pitching wedge he was striking them with uncanny accuracy toward the doorknob of the outer door.

With a twinkle in his eye, he inquired if his golf game was keeping me awake. I assured him that it was not, and spent the rest of the night trying to sleep but really listening for more golf balls to strike the doorknob.

Judge Hugh "Scotty" Campbell

Judge Hugh "Scotty" Campbell of Charlotte was so nicknamed because he had the reputation for squeezing nickels till the buffalos squalled, but I don't remember him for that as much as for his humor in the courtroom. Some way, he could manage to come up with a quip to fit any situation.

I once defended a young man who had three bastardy cases against him at one session of superior court, over which Judge Campbell presided. It was necessary for the three cases to be tried one after the other. They involved three different young women.

I managed to get him acquitted on the first two charges, and Solicitor Thad Bryson called the final case. He said the young man's name and yelled, "Come on up."

We overheard Judge Campbell mutter, "Yeah, come on up, Father of Your Country."

Judge Campbell lived on the outskirts of Charlotte. Holding a session of superior court in Charlotte, he woke up late one morning, jumped into his clothes, and sped toward the courthouse.

He passed through a small community whose only officer of the law was a constable elected part-time by the local citizenry. Observing the judge speeding merrily through his trap, the constable lit out with his blue light on, and ran the judge down in the middle of nowhere.

"Young man," said the judge, "I am Hugh Campbell, senior resident judge of Mecklenburg County, and I am late for court."

"Yeah," said the constable, feeling his authority, certain that he could detect a lying man when he saw one, "an' I'm Napoleon Bonapart. Now, put your hands behind your head."

He slapped the cuffs on Judge Campbell and lodged him in the clink. The judge commenced to holler, and the jailer, thinking him to be just another crying drunk, ignored his screams and threats for more than an hour.

Finally, a young lawyer walked by the judge's cell to visit a client, and saw who was locked up.

"Get me out of this damned place, young man," the judge yelled to the lawyer. "I'm an hour late for court—and I hope the first case has that ignorant son of a bitch of a constable as a witness."

Scotty Campbell tried a case in Jackson County that I will never forget. A young lady of questionable morals indicted a man for rape. I tried the case for the defendant, and put my man on the stand.

He testified that he had invited the young woman and her ten-year-old brother to go night fishing with him on Lake Glenville, and that they had accepted. He said when they got to the lake that the young brother was asleep in

3 • Politickles

Go Right Ahead

R. Gregg Cherry was governor of North Carolina during World War II. He was known as a conservationist governor who husbanded the state's funds with such prudence during the war years when construction and building were at a standstill that the governors who succeeded him had a wealth of funds with which to move forward when restrictions were eased.

Governor Cherry also had a great sense of humor and a quick wit.

When a member of his highway commission died, an eager young politician from the deceased's area approached Cherry at graveside during the funeral.

"Governor," the young man whispered, "I sure would like to take John's place."

The governor replied, without an eyebat's hesitation, "Well, it's all right with me if it's all right with the undertaker."

At times, Cherry's humor was biting. An angry woman cornered him and told him that she wouldn't vote for him again if he were the archangel Gabriel.

"Well then, madam, your problem is solved," Cherry replied. "If I were the archangel Gabriel, you couldn't vote in my precinct!"

Once, during a long and tiring reception at the executive mansion, Congressman Basil L. Whitener remembers a man delaying the receiving line by standing in front of Cherry and repeating, "Governor, you don't know my name, do you?"

Cherry solved the problem by thrusting the man's hand into that of William B. Umstead, who was next in line, and exclaiming, "William, tell this damn fool his name!"

Legends and courtroom tales abound, depicting Cherry's unique flair in trial tactics. Cherry once appealed a guilty verdict against one of his clients to the North Carolina Supreme Court.

On the day for argument, Cherry stood up to make his presentation, and the Chief Justice said, "Governor, we're all pleased to have you with us in Raleigh again."

"Well, if it please the Court," Cherry said, "I'm just here to ask you to correct a bad mistake in the superior court and send this case back for a new trial."

"Governor, we have read the record and the briefs," the chief justice said, "and we intend to do just that."

"I am much obliged to you," Cherry said. "I believe that I will bring you gentlemen some more of my business!"

The Eloquence of Clyde R. Hoey

Governor Clyde R. Hoey had no peer in delivering a political speech. He could hold an audience spellbound for an hour, and make the time seem no more than five minutes.

A gentleman of the old school, Governor Hoey wore a swallowtail coat, cellophane collar, black tie with stick pin, always a carnation in his lapel, and in the 1950s, he sported a long mane of beautiful white hair.

In 1952, I was chairman of the Jackson County Democratic Executive Committee. In the election that fall, Frank Brown of Cullowhee ran for the state legislature on the Democratic ticket. His opponent was Orville Coward, a young Sylva lawyer who had huge family connections.

The Democrats were scared that fall!

As county chairman, I decided we had better call in the big guns, so I secured Governor Hoey as our final rally speaker. People from all over Western North Carolina were invited, and on the day of the rally the school auditorium was filled to capacity and beyond, and more than a thousand people outside listened to Governor Hoey's words over a loudspeaker.

I introduced the governor, who rose and first made a few opening remarks about how glad he was to be with us; then, turning to me, he asked me to stand, and told the group: "You know, my friends, we've got to win this election. I've got to have Frank Brown in Raleigh along with the other Democrats on my team.

"But I want you to know that you have the most *honest* Democratic chairman of any county in this state. Why, only last evening he and your good sheriff, Griffin Middleton, took a flashlight up to the cemetery to see if any absentees had been overlooked on their previous trips.

"The sheriff held the flashlight on the tombrocks and Buchanan took down the names of the prospective voters. By and by, they came to a stone inscribed:

JOHN HENRY HIGGIN BOTTOM

whereupon your good sheriff told Buchanan, 'Hell, Buck, we can get two votes out of this one: John Higgin and Henry Bottom,' to which your honest county chairman, to his everlasting credit, balked.

"Unwilling to do *anything* wrong, Mr. Buchanan spoke right up and said, 'No, Griff—we're going to be honest about this thing: We're not going to vote him but once!' "

That same night, I might add, we came across a tombstone inscribed:

HERE LIES A LAWYER AND A CHRISTIAN GENTLEMAN

Griff spoke up and said, "Buck, there's plenty of room in this graveyard. I wonder why they buried 'em both in the same grave."

The Alien

Shortly before election time a few years ago, a quiet, compassionate man who was as polite as anyone could be, walked the streets of his county seat drumming up support for his candidacy for sheriff. He spoke to everyone and invited all to vote for him.

One morning he encountered a woman he had seen but never met. "Good morning, ma'am," he said. "I am John Smith and I'm running for sheriff. I hope I can count on your vote."

Very sweetly, she replied, "I'm sorry, Mr. Smith. I like your appearance but I can't vote for you. You see, I am an alien."

"Sure am sorry," he said as politely as possible, trying not to let disappointment into his voice, "but I do hope you get to feeling better."

Not Enough

When Senator Sam Ervin ran for the United States Senate for the last time, he walked down the street in his hometown of Morganton one morning, and spied an old gentleman whom he hadn't seen in a while.

Never one to pass up a good conversation, Senator Sam engaged the man, and during their conversation, said, "Well, John, I have decided to run for the Senate again, and I sure hope you're still for me."

"Well, Sam," the old man hedged, "I've always voted fer you, but I just don't know about this time."

Obviously shocked, Senator Sam returned, "But, John, don't you remember that I put your sister in as postmaster five or six years ago?"

"Yeah, I remember that."

"And I got your brother out of the penitentiary three years ago."

"I recollect."

"I put your nephew on my staff two years ago . . ."

"Yep."

". . . and helped your wife with her Social Security problem just six months ago . . ."

"That's right."

". . . and you tell me you don't know whether you can

vote for me again!"

"But, Sam," the old man asked, "what have you done fer me *lately*?"

Poor Shots

During the last year of Richard Nixon's presidency, shortly before he resigned, he had a speaking engagement at the Charlotte Coliseum.

My administrative assistant, Marion Jones, and I were in Charlotte playing golf that day, and being loyal Democrats, we decided we would go to the Coliseum and see how many lies Nixon could tell in thirty minutes.

We found a couple of seats, and thirty minutes later we heard the approaching sirens of the Nixon Imperial Motorcade. Nixon exited his limousine and took his place on the podium.

The local high school band played the national anthem, and then a large cannon was rolled onto the floor just below where Nixon was standing. With the muzzle pointed toward the president, and firing blanks, the cannon boomed out a twenty-one-gun salute.

When the echoes of the twenty-first shot faded away, and Marion saw Nixon still standing at rigid attention, he turned to me and complained:

"Buck—damned if they didn't miss him every time!"

A Pure Case of Slander

A man in Webster was one of Jackson County's most dependable Democrats. He could be depended on to serve as a marker in the elections to help voters who actually needed help in marking their ballots, and also to help those he was able to convince needed help anyway.

He had been marking the ticket of an old man for many years, marking it straight Democratic although the old man was actually a Republican.

The Republican judge of elections in Webster was a devout party woman who watched the polls with an eagle eye—always suspicious that the Democrats would do something wrong.

She had watched this man mark the old man's ballot for years, and finally went to the old man and asked, "Uncle Steve, why is it that you always get that man to mark your ballot instead of me? I know you're a Republican and you want to vote a Republican ticket, don't you?"

"I let him help," the old man said, "because I know he's honest. He knows how I want to vote and he votes me that way."

"Well, let me tell you something," she said. "You watch him this time and see. The Republican column is on the left side of the ballot, and the Democratic column is on the right side. You watch and see if he doesn't mark your ticket on the right."

"I will," said the old man.

He accepted his ballot from the registrar and went into the booth with his marker. Before handing the marker his ticket, however, he told him what the woman had said.

"Damn that woman!" the marker said. "She's always slandering me. You know good and well I'm going to mark this ballot like you want."

So he turned the ticket upside down and marked it on the bottom left.

The old man thanked him for being so honest and went outside and gave the Republican woman hell for maligning his good and honest friend.

Truly a Democrat

The late William "Uncle Bill" Byers was perhaps the strongest Democrat in North Carolina. Born and reared in Haywood County, he cut his teeth on politics before he was old enough to vote, and was active in Democratic circles throughout North Carolina well past his ninetieth year.

He served for more than forty years as a Democratic Presidential Elector, perhaps more times than any other person in history.

Once, during a regular election in Haywood County where Republicans were in short supply, Uncle Bill was asked by a friend if he were such a strong Democrat that he would vote for a yellow dog if its name was on the Democratic ticket.

"Oh, no," Uncle Bill replied, and then after a moment's thought, added, "Not in the primary, at least."

When Hubert Humphrey headed the Democratic ticket as candidate for President of the United States, I was invited to speak to a huge rally in Haywood County.

Our candidates for governor, lieutenant governor, and Congress were there, along with members of the council of state and all county candidates. The rally overflowed the large school auditorium and spilled out into the hallways where amplifiers were hastily set up so everyone could hear.

During that election, there was much criticism of Mr. Humphrey, and, quite frankly, the state and local candidates played him down and used his name infrequently in their campaigns.

During my talk, unfortunately acceding to the wishes of our other candidates, I did not dwell on the national ticket.

After I had spoken and received polite applause, the master of ceremonies called upon that venerable and beloved old gentleman, Uncle Bill Byers, to make a few comments.

I can remember the resonant voice of that man in his nineties, which literally boomed across that assembled group.

"I am ashamed," he said, "that all of our candidates from the statehouse to the courthouse have spoken this evening and that none—yes, not a single one—has mentioned the name of that great senator, the titular head of our National Democratic Party and the man to whom we will all have to look for leadership in this troubled period—the name of a great leader, a great Christian, and of a good man: Hubert Horatio Humphrey, our candidate for President of these United States."

As he turned toward his seat, the entire audience rose in unison and began to sing that old rallying song, "Happy Days Are Here Again."

When the rally finally broke up after at least ten minutes of singing and cheering for Uncle Bill, he could not leave the room for more than an hour while candidates and Democrats in attendance shook his hand and pledged their support for our presidential ticket.

Uncle Bill was once sitting on his porch when a young lad of about ten walked by with a covered wicker basket.

Knowing the youngster was a neighbor boy, Uncle Bill asked what he had in the basket.

"My old cat gave birth to five kittens," the lad replied. "I'm a-showing them off."

He showed them to Uncle Bill, who, knowing the boy's family as staunch Democrats, asked, "What do you reckon those cats' politics is?"

Uncle Bill was somewhat chagrined when the lad replied, "They look to me like they're Republicans."

About ten days later, however, the same boy dropped by to see Uncle Bill.

"I think," said the boy, "that I made a mistake about the kittens' being Republican. I think they're actually Democrats."

"What makes you think that?" Uncle Bill asked, and he forever afterward had a soft spot in his heart for that young man, who replied, "Because now they have their eyes open."

Old-Timey Politics

One of the great mountain solicitors figured he could do just about anything he wanted while in office—and usually did. He held office during the days when the solicitor was a much more powerful man than he is today.

Once, when running for reelection he became concerned over his chances. He traveled to the district's largest town and contacted the chief of police who was also a close personal friend.

The solicitor pleaded his case. "I shore need your help. I've got two good men running agin' me, and frankly, I've got to beat 'em both the first time around. I ain't got the money for a second primary."

"Mr. Solicitor," drawled the police chief, "we've allus been good friends; our pappies was good friends, and our grandpappies, too, I reckon. I've allus supported you, and will agin, but to get the votes of some of the low-down people I know, you gotta give me something to bargain with."

The solicitor thought a moment. "I'm still the solicitor," he said, "and I guess they'll most be on my docket after the election—so promise 'em any damn thing you want to."

The police chief went to work, and the solicitor won reelection. At the next session of court, the solicitor was given a list of thirty drunken drivers whose cases he should dismiss because they had supported him for reelection.

True to his word, the solicitor dismissed every case.

In those days, a conviction for driving while intoxicated carried an automatic suspension of driving privileges for twelve months, and there were no "limited driving privileges" as we have now, which permit a person to drive to and from work.

Ten days after the commissioner of motor vehicles in Raleigh was notified of the dismissals, he wrote the solicitor, listed the cases by number and name, and asked for a reason for dismissal in each case.

The cantankerous old solicitor read the letter, turned it over, and wrote in longhand on the back: "Dear Mr. Commissioner: There were three reasons I dismissed these cases, and the same reasons apply to all. They are (1) the defendants wanted them dismissed; (2) I wanted to dismiss them; and (3) I could dismiss them. Very truly yours."

He never heard from the cases again.

Nip and Tuck

John Barleycorn, a former high official, like all of us, had some weaknesses, and one of his was that he sometimes loved to take more than a nip. Never, however, did he ever permit booze to interfere with the faithful and unswerving devotion to his duties.

Following his term of office, he returned to his home town to practice law. A stranger came to town in need of legal advice in a rather complicated lawsuit. Since he knew no one, he went to the office of the clerk of court and discreetly inquired who was the best lawyer in town.

"That's John Barleycorn, when he's sober," the clerk answered.

"Well, who's the next best?"

"John Barleycorn when he's drunk."

Yes, He's Positive

Zebulon B. Vance is best remembered as North Carolina's Civil War governor. An able lawyer and politician who served the bar in Buncombe County for many years, Vance eventually served as a member of the United States Senate.

Vance had a positive aura about him. He had the

great trait of being able to transmit his positiveness to the people.

Never in his career was he more positive than one morning on the floor of the United States Senate when he rose to argue against building a bridge over a certain stream.

For thirty minutes, Senator Vance gave a passionate plea against building the bridge, then after pausing for emphasis, he sallied forth with his parting blast:

"Mr. Speaker," he said, "they don't really need a bridge across that stream. It isn't a large enough stream to merit a bridge. Why, Mr. Speaker, I can pee halfway across that stream."

The Speaker banged his gavel for order. "Sit down, Mr. Vance," he shouted, "you are out of order!"

When the uproar quieted, Vance intoned, "I know it, Mr. Speaker. I know I was out of order. Why, if I was in order, I could pee *all* the way across that little stream."

Sheriff of "Bloody Madison"

Since the memory of man runneth not to the contrary, E. Y. Ponder has been sheriff of Madison County—"Bloody Madison," as it is known along the ridgelines of Western North Carolina.

Throughout the width and breadth of North Carolina, E. Y. Ponder is known as one of the finest law officials in the state, particularly in the realm of investigation and in the manner in which he treats the people of his county.

E. Y. has a single little office in the courthouse in Marshall where he "holds court" with the people of Madison County, witnesses, defendants, lawyers, and all of his friends who drop in to see him.

He knows every man, woman, and child in Madison County by appearance, by name, and by reputation.

I went to see E. Y. once on a political matter. He was alone in his office, reared back in the chair behind his desk, his feet on the desk, his hat on his head.

We discussed the matter I had come to see him about. It was a cold winter day and his office was warm and cozy. We began to swap yarns and talk about general things in general terms.

His telephone rang. When he answered, I could hear only his end of the conversation. I pieced together the story from E. Y.'s questions and answers.

A reputable citizen who lived about twenty miles from Marshall had just shot and killed a neighbor. The citizen was on the phone, telling E. Y. what he had done.

The sheriff listened patiently, and then said, "Well, John, just come on in to the office. I'll have to have a warrant issued, so bring somebody who can make your bond."

He hung up, shook his head in dismay, and told me the gist of the conversation. Thirty minutes later, a pickup truck stopped in front of the courthouse and the man who had done the killing walked into E. Y. Ponder's office, accompanied by his wife, his son, and his daughter-in-law.

E. Y. excused himself and took the man to the magistrate's office where he took out the warrant, and the man made bond and left.

Some months later, a jury acquitted the man on the grounds of self-defense.

This story does not indicate any indifference on the part of E. Y. Ponder to the killing of a fellow human being and the enforcement of the law, but rather indicates the ability of Sheriff Ponder to size up a defendant, to know what the defendant will do and what he will not do.

Had this man been an outlaw, E. Y. Ponder would have gone out, probably alone, and taken him into custody at the scene. But he knew the man, he knew he was a man of his word, and if he said he would come in, he would most certainly come in.

Sheriff Ponder treated the man as any man would like to be treated—and the defendant showed E. Y. the respect of his position and his office.

Harmless Old Coot

Once when Mary Faye Brumby of Murphy, the seat of Cherokee County, ran for the North Carolina State Senate with strong Republican opposition, she had to campaign in four counties: Cherokee, Swain, Jackson, and Transylvania.

Before the general election, Mary Faye and her husband, Ed, attended the Vance-Aycock dinner in Asheville, and a number of political figures from Western North Carolina were in my room. Included were Mrs. Brumby and Floyd Woody of Haywood County. Floyd was a crusty old politician in his early eighties.

He and Mary Faye got into a conversation regarding her race, in which Mary Faye stated that she knew very few people in Transylvania County and would like to have someone who was acquainted over there take her around to meet the political leaders and voters.

Floyd quickly volunteered. "I would be delighted," he said, "if you would come over and pick me up in Waynesville and we could go to Transylvania together. If you could spend two or three days and nights with me in Transylvania County, I could introduce you to most of the people."

Realizing exactly what he had said, Floyd reddened a bit and added, "You can tell your husband not to worry a damned bit, because at my age I've been dehorned."

The Other Choice

Harry Truman walked through the Democratic National Convention in 1948, drumming up support for his incumbent bid for the presidency. He asked a delegate from North Carolina if he could count on his support.

"Mr. Truman," said the delegate, truthfully, "I would not vote for you if you were the last man on earth."

Truman turned to an aide. "Put that man down as doubtful," he said.

Truman saw two more delegates in deep conversation, and when he eavesdropped he heard one say, "Truman is my last choice."

The other delegate asked, "Who is your first choice?"

The first replied, "Anyone."

A Matter of Observation

As a good and lifelong Democrat, I have always heard that there are a number of ways to tell when a Republican is lying:

If you look at his ears and if they wiggle a bit, that's a good indication that he is telling a lie.

If you are not certain from this, however, you can watch

his nose, and if his nose twitches, that's another indication that he is lying.

However, if, after both of these tests, you are still uncertain, you should observe his mouth: If his mouth is open, then you will know for sure that he is lying.

Threatened

Genevieve Vetoe has never had any particular trouble with her name since she married Frank Vetoe a few years ago.

Folks kidded her about her new name and usually made up funny stories about it, concerning certain things in Washington.

Genevieve had never made jokes about the name until one morning when she read the front page of *The Asheville Citizen*.

"Frank," she screamed, "what have you done?"

Frank came running.

"What's the matter?" he said. "What's the matter?"

She pointed to the headline which read, "Carter Threatens Vetoes."

"I thought he was going to choke me," she said, "but then he started to laugh."

She'll be careful with her jokes from now on.

A Man's Rights

Zeno Ponder, the Madison County political boss, once said that he and a "few of the boys" were up in the graveyard one night taking down the names of some potential voters when one of the fellows called, "Mr. Ponder, come over here a minute."

When Zeno reached the man, the fellow said, "I've been scratching this tombstone ten minutes, Mr. Ponder, and I can't make out this man's name."

"Just keep scratching, son," Zeno said. "That man's got as much right to vote as any man up here!"

A Couple of Votes

I had announced and filed as incumbent for the office of Thirtieth District solicitor, subject to the Democratic Primary in May of 1982. There was a young attorney from one of the smaller counties in the seven-county district who began nosing around for support enough to take me on.

Not being very well known in Cherokee County, he decided to talk with my good friend Blaine Stalcup, the high sheriff of Cherokee County.

He told Blaine of his intentions and asked how Blaine thought he would do in Cherokee if he ran.

Blaine ruminated for a moment or two, then asked the young man if he were married.

"Yes, I'm married," he replied. "Why?"

"Well," Stalcup said, "if you and your wife move out here in time to register, you'll get two votes!"

End of my opposition from that young man!

4 • *Here Lies a Squire!*

Smartest Man

Although he wasn't overly well educated, "Uncle" Jim Turpin of Sylva was one of the smartest men in Western North Carolina. He had what the mountaineer likes to call "horse sense."

Jim held many positions of responsibility in public life, including alderman for the Town of Waynesville, police chief of Waynesville, police chief of Sylva, superintendent of a state prison camp, and in his latter years the Sylva Justice of the Peace. In all of these positions, he applied liberal doses of "horse sense" to his work.

When he was superintendent of the Jackson County prison camp, which had two long, single-story cellblocks, he liked nothing more on a balmy night than to slip up to the windows and eavesdrop on the prisoners.

One August night he overheard a conversation between two prisoners. One, who was planning an escape attempt, said to the other, "Do you know where I'm going to be next Saturday night? I'm going to be lying on my sweetheart's divan with my head in her lap, and I'm going to be saying to her, 'Be careful, honey, when you pick them blackheads out of my nose.'"

The other replied, "Well, that shows you don't know Jim Turpin! Next Saturday night, you're really gonna be lying flat on your belly on the cold concrete and that old prison doctor, Grover Wilkes, is going to be saying to you, 'Lay still, you son of a bitch, so's I can pick that buckshot out of your ass!' "

Is Orville Right?

Uncle Jim was a justice of the peace for a number of years and a stalwart Democrat all his life. I had appointed him to the justice's seat when I was in the state legislature, and when I returned to my law practice, his office was next to mine.

In addition to hearing very minor criminal cases, he also had authority to hear civil matters up to fifty dollars.

Once, two neighbors in Cashiers got into a row about which one owned a certain something, and one brought suit against the other.

Orville Coward, a Sylva attorney who was as staunch a Republican as Uncle Jim and I were Democrats—and, may I add, a very close friend of mine—was retained by one of the parties, and I by the other. The case was to be heard by Uncle Jim.

On the morning of the hearing, Orville and I, and our clients, met in Uncle Jim's office. I had nothing with me but a pencil and a yellow legal pad (I thought I should take *something*) and Orville came equipped with a half-dozen volumes of the *Supreme Court Reporter.*

We put our evidence before the justice, I spoke a few words about why I felt my client ought to prevail, and then Orville read law from the Supreme Court decisions for about thirty minutes—with Uncle Jim staring at him blankly.

When we finished and rested our cases, Uncle Jim got up and asked me to step out into the hall with him before he ruled.

When we were out of Orville's hearing, he whispered, "Now, Buck, course you *know* I'm agonna rule for you—but, by God, tell me the truth: Is Orville right?"

I Swear by Webster's

After Turpin had been justice of the peace for about ten years and had sworn witnesses on a book with the cover off it all during that time, one day when I was in his office telling jokes I idly picked up his "swearing book," flipped through it, and made the amazing discovery that all that time he had been swearing witnesses on *Webster's International Dictionary.*

Thinking it over, I concluded that it really didn't matter as long as nobody knew the difference.

That's the way Uncle Jim felt, for when I called it to his attention, he said, "It don't make no difference. A good man is going to tell the truth sworn or unsworn, and a crook is going to swear a lie anyhow!"

He always said, "You know, Buck, there's more damned lies sworn in the courtroom than in the tax office."

Fudged a Little

A justice of the peace was empowered by law to marry folks, but Uncle Jim didn't know that when he asked me to appoint him. In fact, when he asked me to make him a justice of the peace through the legislature, he gave as his only reason for wanting the position the fact that when he died they could chisel on his tombrock, "Here Lies a Squire!"

A few weeks after his appointment, he came running into my office scared to death. "Buck," he said, "I'm in one helluva mess. They's a young couple in my office wanting me to marry 'em."

"So?" I looked at him, trying not to laugh.

"Well, first, can I legally do it? And second, how in the hell *do* I do it?"

I calmed him down and told him what to do: "Just have them stand before you and take each other's right hand. Then you ask, 'Do you, John, take this woman to be your lawful wedded wife, to live together in holy matrimony until death do you part?' and so on." I went through the whole ritual with him. "Then you solemnly say, 'Now, by the authority vested in me by the State of North Carolina, I pronounce you husband and wife.' That's all there is to it."

Somewhat relieved, but obviously not entirely, he asked if I would go into his office with him, stand behind him, and keep him straight through the ceremony.

In we went, and there sat two teenagers, the boy no more than eighteen, and the girl pushing sixteen. I positioned myself behind Uncle Jim but because of his desire to get through the ceremony quickly, I didn't get to coach him a bit.

In an unusually gruff voice, he ordered, "STAND UP!" They stood. He told them how to hold hands, then spoke to the boy: "Do you take this woman fer your wife?"

"I do!"

Turning to the girl, he bellowed, "Do you take this boy fer your man?"

"I do!"

"Okay," he said, "your knot's tied." He turned to me with the license in his hand. "Buck, where do I sign this damned thing?" I showed him and he fixed his signature to the license.

That was about three in the afternoon. Around nine that evening, someone knocked timidly on my door. I answered, and there in the cold evening stood the young couple, twisting and squirming on one foot and then the other.

"Are you Mr. Buchanan?" the boy asked.

"I am."

"The same laywer who was at Justice of the Peace Turpin's this afternoon?"

"Yes."

"Well," he squirmed, "we were going to honeymoon in Gatlinburg, so we drove over there and had supper and checked into a motel. But we just couldn't go to bed comfortably without coming back to see you. Now you're a lawyer, and I want you to tell me the truth: Are we shore 'nuff married?"

"Young man," I assured him, "with the signature of the justice on your certificate, and those of the witnesses, of which I was one, you're married just as good as if you'd done it in the First Baptist Church."

"Thank God," said the obviously relieved young man, "because we really fudged a little *before* we got to Gatlinburg!"

First Up

Jim Turpin lived about a mile from his office. He had glaucoma which gave him "tunnel vision"—he could see only straight ahead. In walking between office and home, he passed Cogdill Motor Company, which had a filling station next to it with an old-fashioned grease pit, a concrete hole in the ground about four feet wide, eight feet long, and six feet deep. The mechanic worked on the underside of cars from this hole.

One day about noon, with the sun shining directly into the pit, Uncle Jim, heading home, misjudged the distance from the pit, and stepped right into it.

He thudded to the bottom, landed on his back, and was stunned senseless. When he woke up, he saw the beautiful white clouds passing overhead, framed in the top of the pit, and remarked to himself, "Well, old man, hit's judgment day and you're the first one up!"

Seed It Alike

When in his seventies, Uncle Jim rode with me to Asheville one day. Enroute, we came to an intersection with a stop sign requiring me to stop before crossing. Absorbed in conversation, I drove straight through the sign, and as I glanced to my right there was the biggest truck I ever saw bearing down on us.

I cut to the left, stepped on the gas, and the truck cleared us by a cat's whisker. Shaking and scared to death, I stopped the car, gripped the steering wheel, and broke out into a cold sweat that matched the sweat Uncle Jim had already generated.

In a shaky voice, he said, "Buck, you damned near got us killed—but let me tell you, if he had hit us, I'd of seed it just like you!"

Too Many

Many years ago when Jim Turpin lived in Haywood County, he threw his hat in the ring for a part-time commissioner's seat. A few days before the primary, he met an old gentleman, a friend of his, on the street in Waynesville. The old man commented on Jim's race, asked him how he was making out, and hit him for the loan of a quarter to get him something to eat.

"Old man," Jim said, "I don't have a quarter." That was probably the truth.

"Well, I was planning to vote for you," the old man said, "but if you're going to be so damned tight, I guess I'll not."

"That's all right," said Jim, stung to the core. "I've got more votes now than I need, and I'm letting 'em off."

The primary came—and Jim got beat. A few days later, he met his old friend in town again.

"What happened, Jim?" the old fellow asked. "You told me you had too many votes and was letting 'em off."

"That's the trouble," Jim responded. "I let too damned many off!"

Aging Process

Uncle Jim and I were talking once about the qualities of the various brands of liquor, including our mountain corn.

He told me he had heard that liquor improved with age.

"Yes," I said, "I believe some of the distilleries age their spirits."

"Well, I don't believe it helps a bit," he said. "I kept some overnight one time and couldn't tell a bit of difference the next day."

Chief Justice

White-maned Uncle Jim could have passed himself off as Speaker of the House anywhere in the country when he dressed up in his blue serge suit and red necktie.

He was wearing that outfit one evening when I drove him from Raleigh to Sylva. We were somewhere around Statesville when Uncle Jim said, "Buck, ain't you gonna stop nowhere and eat nothing? My stomach's been a-growling for twenty minutes."

I drove on for four or five miles and came to a decent-looking restaurant, and as I pulled into the parking lot I made up my mind to have a little fun.

"Uncle Jim," I said, "with the shape your stomach's in, you stay in the car and I'll go in and see if they've got anything decent that your ulcers can handle."

"All right, Buck," he said, "but try to make it rare roast beef."

I asked for the manager and when he came up, I said, "I am Mr. Johnson, administrative assistant to Walter P. Stacy, the Chief Justice of the North Carolina Supreme Court." (There had been a Chief Justice Walter P. Stacy, but he had died twenty-five or thirty years previously.)

"I am taking the chief justice to the mountains for his health," I went on, "and he is waiting in the car to see if you have anything that he can eat, preferably rare roast beef."

The manager assured me that he had some of the finest roast beef in that part of the state, and we could have it as rare as we desired.

So far, so good. I figured Uncle Jim would be easy to pawn off as the chief justice if I could keep his mouth shut when anyone was around, especially the manager. One peep out of Uncle Jim that the manager could hear, and the jig would be up.

"The chief justice," I said, "is suffering from a nervous disorder, and would appreciate it if you could seat him in a private corner somewhere, away from anyone else."

"Most certainly," replied the manager. "Just give me about five minutes, please."

I went back to the car, and in five minutes brought Uncle Jim in. He certainly had a stately look about him.

Everybody bowed and scraped when Uncle Jim entered, and he gave me a curious glance. I shrugged, and ushered him to the table the manager pointed out, a small table for two in a private room, set with china plates, sterling silver, and crystal goblets on a white linen tablecloth.

"Just don't say anything," I told him when we were seated. "I have already ordered."

Soon, the manager himself brought in two platters of rare roast beef with plenty of vegetables, and a glass of iced tea for me and sweet milk for Uncle Jim.

From that point on, Uncle Jim was too busy to talk, and we enjoyed one of the finest meals I have ever eaten on the road. When we finished, I hustled Uncle Jim out of there and into the car, and went back to pay the bill.

The manager would have no money, however. "No, sir,"

he said. "It's an honor to serve the chief justice."

"But he is a very wealthy man," I lied, "and he insists on paying for his meal."

The manager would not take a penny.

Finally, I gave up and thanked him profusely and went out to the car, sorry that the joke had backfired. I *had* intended to pay for the meal.

I drove ten miles up the road, and Uncle Jim said, "Buck, I never et in a place like that. Did you see the service we got? And them was undoubtedly the finest rations I ever et! I'm a-going to stop there every time I pass that place, and eat."

I spoke up right quick. "Uncle Jim, you've stopped at that place your last time." Then I told him what I had done and how the joke had backfired.

He didn't laugh, and I could tell he was mulling my story over. In a minute, he said, "Buck, speed up and let's get back in my jurisdiction. Damned if we ain't frauded that feller!"

5 • Law and Order

His Legend Will Never Die

Jesse James Bailey was the legendary sheriff of "Bloody Madison" from 1920 to 1922, at the height of prohibition.

He would be the first to say that "legendary" was a big word to hang on any man, but it fit him like a glove.

He was later sheriff of Buncombe County from 1928 to 1930, and for decades after that (he lived to be ninety-two) he worked as chief detective for Southern Railway. He was a legendary yarn-spinner who captivated thousands of audiences with his tales of mirth.

You could always tell when Jesse stretched the truth by the twinkle in his eyes.

One thing that made Jesse such a great storyteller was the music in his bones. He came by music honestly. He was a nephew of Fiddlin' Bill Hensley, who sawed a legend of his own on a priceless Jacobus Stainer made in Germany soon after the Civil War.

Jesse got the fiddle after Fiddlin' Bill's death and prized it as much as he did Jimmie Rodgers' guitar.

Rodgers, the "Singing Brakeman," worked as a brakeman for Southern in Asheville for about a year in the middle 1920s, and when he was fired for drinking he moved on and left the guitar behind. It came into Jesse's possession and old Jesse considered it a valuable instrument when Rodgers landed in Nashville and became the "Father of Country Music."

Born in 1888 in the wilds of Madison County, Jesse was named not for the infamous Missouri outlaw but for his grandfathers, Jesse Hensley and James Jefferson Bailey.

But Jesse even colored up that story. He said his father, Erasmus (Dink) Bailey, was working in the fields a week after Jesse was born when a Bible-selling preacher came by and asked Dink if he'd like to buy a new Bible.

"Bible?" Dink said. "What's a Bible?"

"You mean to say you don't know what the Good Book is?" the preacher asked.

"Well, I've got one book," Dink said, "but that ain't it. I've got a book about the life of the James boys of Missouri."

The preacher struck a deal. He left a Bible with Dink and told him to read it. He'd be back in a few days and if Dink liked the Bible he could pay for it. If he didn't like it, the preacher would take it back and there would be no charge.

A week later, the preacher returned and asked Dink how he liked the Bible.

"It's a dandy," Dink said. "Them James boys was wild, but they couldn't hold a candle to Samson and the Philistine boys. I'll buy your book."

"I reckon," Jesse James Bailey said, "that if I'd been born a week after I was, I'd abin named Samson Philistine Bailey."

Jesse said he started running for sheriff in 1896. "I was eight years old," he said, "when Sheriff J. H. White and a posse came by our house about dark, looking for a man. The sheriff got off his horse and talked to my daddy for awhile and when he got back on he dropped his pistol. It was full dark then and nobody noticed the pistol till my daddy found it the next morning. I thought it was the prettiest pistol I'd ever seen, and I made up my mind right then I'd run for sheriff some day, so's I could carry a pistol like that."

The Volstead Act went into force in 1919 and prohibition was at its height in 1920 when the "dry" forces of Madison County elected Republican Jesse James Bailey sheriff.

"I went around to all the moonshiners," Jesse said, "and asked for their support. I told 'em I wouldn't do 'em no harm unless they built their stills out in the road where I'd stub my toe over them. But they said no, they couldn't support me. They said they knew what the other man would do, but they didn't know me that well.

"I'd never touched a drop of whiskey," Jesse said. "Still haven't. And when the dry people voted me in, I vowed to dry up Madison County. I went in arunnin' the blockaders and I come out arunnin' 'em. I didn't dry the county up, but in two years I raised the price of whiskey from fifteen dollars a gallon to seventy-five. I made it scarce."

The job of sheriff at that time was a wild and dangerous occupation. Madison's roads were primitive and the sheriff had to go by horseback where he couldn't take the train. Jesse was a flamboyant man who wore his pistol low on his hip so he could pull it quicker. He rode a big horse with a smooth gait that could put the miles away with ease.

Jesse put mirth behind him when he went out to

enforce the law, and his battles with Madison's moon-shiners, especially with Doyle and Jesse Massey, the sons of Red Jim Massey of the Little Pine section, became legendary.

Their combat was like the pages of a wild western. Jesse Massey killed one of Bailey's deputies, and Bailey vowed to bring him in. When the smoke of their battle cleared, both Massey boys were behind bars for murder.

Jesse poked a lot of fun at the sheriff's office. "When I was runnin', " he said, "I needed every vote I could get. I went up to a preacher one day and asked him if I could depend on his support. About that time the preacher's little boy picked up a cigarette butt and started to put it in his pocket. The preacher saw him and said, 'Put that thing down, you little runt. Next thing you know, you'll be runnin' for sheriff.' I shut up because I figured there wasn't no way I could get that preacher's vote."

Jesse was an old-time lawman, no question of that. A few years ago he said he didn't think he could be a lawman today.

"It's changed too much," he said. "When you go after a feller with a warrant you've got to take a Baby Ruth candy bar in your pocket and when you catch him you've got to say, 'Excuse me, sir, but I have a warrant for your arrest. I also have a candy bar for you which you can eat while I go find you a lawyer. Don't tell me nothing and don't tell nobody else nothing till you talk to your lawyer.'

"In my day," he said, "you went up to a man and knocked him down and if he got up you said, 'I've got a warrant for you. You're under arrest.' You couldn't mollycoddle them fellers if you wanted to stay sheriff long."

Justice Prevailed

A woman driving a Buick stopped on Battery Park Avenue in Asheville during Christmas's heaviest traffic rush and waited while another car backed out of a parking space. Before she could get into the place, however, a Volkswagen whipped around her and into the parking place.

The woman stopped her engine, put on the emergency brake, got out of the car, and walked over to the VW, tapping on the window. The man rolled down the window, and BLAM! the woman socked him in the nose with her fist.

A moment later the VW was gone and the woman's Buick occupied the parking space.

Justice, apparently, had prevailed.

The Snuff Box Evidence

Warfield Turpin was a deputy sheriff and jailer under three successive sheriffs in Jackson County. Despite his lack of formal education, Warfield had an intuitive sense that made him a fine officer.

Warfield often turned his sense of humor on himself, stating on more than one occasion that "I'm the most level-headed man in the sheriff's department. When I dip snuff and stand level with the ground, I am so level-headed that snuff runs out both sides of my mouth at the same time."

A man whom we shall call "Howell" for anonymity lived in a remote section of Jackson County some time ago. He was a prince of a fellow who sometimes depended on the manufacture of corn whiskey for his living. He made only good liquor, and never sold it to children or drunks. He traded mostly with doctors, lawyers, judges, businessmen, and other upright citizens.

Because of these attributes, Howell's whiskey endeavors went largely ignored for many years until a neighbor had a falling-out with him and insisted that the law take a closer look at Howell.

Unable to ignore the complaints, the sheriff and Warfield Turpin drove to Howell's house one afternoon to place him under arrest.

Howell's house was small and had no indoor plumbing. He had arranged a drain pipe from his kitchen sink to run under the floor, past the front steps, and down the approach trail to the house.

Howell spied the sheriff and deputy coming up the trail and immediately rushed to the kitchen and poured all the spirits he had on hand down the drain. Then he answered the sheriff's knock and let him in. The sheriff had posted Warfield on the path to the house about twenty feet from the front steps.

The moment the sheriff stepped in the front door, he smelled the odor of Howell's pure, double-distilled liquor, but found none for evidence.

At his station, Warfield observed a clear fluid pouring from the end of the drain pipe and smelled the odor of corn juice. He had nothing in his pockets that would hold liquid—except a Bruton's snuff can. Quickly he fished it out, emptied the snuff on the ground, except for a sizeable portion which he dumped inside his lower lip, and then caught the snuff can full of whiskey and put the cap on it.

Howell's trial was a scream. He's the only man I remember having been convicted on a snuff box full of evidence. The judge gave him a suspended sentence and

116

a low-voiced admonition to continue to refrain from selling his stuff to minors and drunks.

It's Habit-Forming

In 1971, Union County District Criminal Court was in session in the old courthouse in Monroe. Judge Walter M. Lampley presided over the session, and before him one morning stood a vagrant who had come through Monroe a week previously and had stolen a coat from a parked automobile.

Nabbed by the Monroe police, the defendant had spent a week in jail before electing to go into court and plead guilty "to get it over with as quickly as possible," he said.

Judge Lampley accepted the plea, heard the evidence from the state, sentenced the defendant to the number of days he had already spent in jail, gave him credit for time served, and sent him on his way.

The defendant thanked the court politely, backed out through the gate in the rail, turned and went down the aisle, and as he got to the back door of the courtroom reached over and plucked a police officer's coat off the coat rack and went on out into the hall.

He was apprehended before he got out of the courthouse and by sundown was roosting in the same cell that he had begun the day in.

The Neighborhood Watch

The Neighborhood Watch Program really works.
Ask Boyd Simmons. He'll tell you how well it works.

Folks in his section of Asheville—Montford Hills—are a neighborly group. They keep a close watch on each other's homes and, in accordance with the stipulations of the Neighborhood Watch Program, report any suspicious activity to the police.

On a recent day, Simmons had a lot of things to do. His wife, Oralene, went to work as usual, and he busied himself getting the chores done.

By mid-afternoon he'd finished his work around the house. A man drove up in a van, parked in front of the Simmons home, and came inside to repair the furnace. Simmons telephoned Oralene and told her he was going to take the car to the shop and have some repairs made. He said he wouldn't be home when she got there, that he would stay at the garage until the car was finished. He didn't mention the furnace repairman.

At the garage, however, the mechanic said he would need a couple of hours to make the repairs, and Simmons said he'd come back for it, since he didn't want to wait that long.

He walked home. It wasn't far. The streets in the Montford Hills area wind around the contours of the hills, and Simmons took a short cut through the woods. He approached his house from the road out of the woods.

He reached in his pocket for the door key, and remembered he'd left it on the key ring at the garage. "No matter," he told himself. "I'll crawl in the window."

About that time, Mrs. Clay Roberts, a neighbor, looked out her window, through the woods, and saw a man crawling through a basement window at the Simmons' home. She called the police.

When Simmons got inside the house, the furnace repairman was still there. He was finished, but had to carry out some tools and broken parts of the furnace. Simmons gave him a hand.

The telephone rang, and Simmons answered it. It was another neighbor, Elrita Nesbitt, calling to see what time Oralene would pick her up for a meeting they were to attend later on.

"I don't know," Simmons said. "She isn't home yet."

Suddenly, a police car whizzed past Elrita's house. It was followed closely by another. Both had sirens going, blue lights flashing.

"Here comes a police car, fast," Elrita said.

"I hear it," Simmons said.

"Wonder what's going on?" Elrita said.

"Nothing over here," Simmons said. . . . "Wait a minute. They're knocking on my door."

He put the phone down, and Elrita could hear the police pounding on his door. She pressed the phone tighter to her ear. She could hear loud voices.

Simmons came back to the phone. "I've got to go now, Elrita," he said. "They think I broke into my own house and am stealing my furniture."

He hung up.

About the time Elrita called Simmons, the telephone rang at the Livingston Street Community Center, and Oralene Simmons answered it. Mrs. Roberts was on the line.

"Is anybody at home at your house?" Mrs. Roberts asked.

"No," Oralene said. "My husband is at the garage having his car fixed. Is anything wrong?"

"You'd better believe something's wrong," Mrs. Roberts said. "I saw a man climb in a window and he and another man are carrying out your furniture. I called the police."

"Lord have mercy!" Oralene shouted. She hung up, grabbed her coat, ran out and jumped in her car, and headed home—fast.

She blasted through town with her emergency lights flashing, blowing her horn. Traffic moved over and let her by. She blew past a police car going down Montford. It, too, pulled over and let her go.

Approaching her house, she saw four police cruisers, blue lights flashing, the paddy wagon, and a van parked in her drive. She jammed on the brakes, skidded to a stop, leaped out of the car, and ran to the house.

An officer met her in the front yard.

"Mrs. Simmons?" he asked.

"Yes," she said, "I'm Mrs. Simmons."

"There is a man in your house who says he's your husband. He was carrying things out of the house."

"He's not *my* husband," Mrs. Simmons said. "*My* husband is at the garage with his car."

They walked in the house. In the livingroom, Boyd Simmons sat sheepishly in a chair, surrounded by half a dozen tough-looking police officers. The furnace repairman was there, too.

She gasped. "He *is* my husband," she said.

"Of course, I'm your husband," he bristled. "Will you tell these officers I'm not stealing my own furniture."

"Did you climb in the window?" she asked.

"I'm inside, aren't I?" he said. "Yes, I climbed in the window. I left my door key at the shop."

"Officers," she said, "there's been a mistake. This is my husband, and he can explain all this—I hope."

"That's all right, ma'am," an officer said.

"I'm sorry," she said.

"Forget it," the officer said. "Better safe than sorry."

The police apologized to Simmons, and left.

When things quieted down, Mrs. Roberts came over from next door. She was horrified to learn she'd called the police on Mr. Simmons.

"I was only trying to watch your house," Mrs. Roberts said.

"I appreciate it," said Mrs. Simmons. "And I will appreciate it if you'll keep watching it."

As an afterthought, she added, "The next time you see someone climbing in the window, it'll be a real burglar, because I'm going to see that my husband carries his door key separate from his car keys."

It was nice to know, Oralene observed later, that the Neighborhood Watch Program works so well.

Her husband had no comment.

The Execution of Curtis Shedd

Curtis Shedd, a Georgian who was as black-hearted a villain as ever I knew, visited relatives in Macon County in the 1950s when Thad Bryson of Bryson City was solicitor.

Shedd took his nine-year-old twin nephews into the remote woods of Macon County, committed a crime against nature on them, bound them to a tree, and left them. They starved to death and their skeletons were later found, still tied to the tree.

Shedd went back to Georgia that same day and shot and killed an uncle with whom he had had a land dispute.

Georgia authorities picked him up on the murder of his uncle, and he also confessed to his heinous North Carolina crime.

At that time, Georgia still used the electric chair for

executions, and North Carolina employed the gas chamber.

Realizing that because of the sheer brutality of the North Carolina crimes, the chance of getting the death penalty was greater here than in Georgia, the Georgia authorities welcomed a visit by Solicitor Bryson and the sheriff of Macon County to interview Shedd and try to persuade him to voluntarily return with them to Macon County for trial.

After talking with Shedd for some time and telling him how much nicer the North Carolina jail facilities were than those of Georgia, Thad popped the question to Shedd about returning to North Carolina with them.

Not knowledgeable in the law, and especially about the means of execution in North Carolina, Shedd commented, "If I thought they wouldn't electrocute me in North Carolina, I'd go back with you right now."

Thad Bryson seized the opportunity. "Curtis," he said, "I can promise you on my word of honor as a gentleman and as solicitor that if you come back with me, you will *not* be electrocuted."

Shedd returned to Macon County, and after a prompt and speedy trial was one of the last death row inmates to be executed in the North Carolina gas chamber before the supreme court held our death penalty law unconstitutional.

Collecting a Debt

Herman Edwards began his law practice in Bryson City in 1946. One day when he was idling around the office with little to do, Bill Wright strolled in and said, "Herman, the *Knoxville Journal* owes me sixty dollars and won't pay. I want you to get my money for me."

Herman explained the difficulty of suing the *Knoxville Journal* in North Carolina since the *Journal* did not operate its business in this state, but Bill countered with the information that occasionally the *Journal* sent one of its trucks into Swain County.

Herman said there might be a possibility of attaching the truck and told Bill to contact him later if he observed one of the newspaper's trucks in the county.

A few months later, Herman's telephone rang at three o'clock one Sunday morning, and Bill told the sleepy attorney, "Wake up, Herman, I just seen that truck downtown. Could you come down and get me some papers?"

Herman told Bill to get a justice of the peace and a deputy sheriff and to meet him in his office in fifteen minutes. The attorney dressed quickly, went to his office, and filled out a form used for filing suit in the justice of the peace court for collection of a debt with attachment proceedings. He gave the papers to Bill and went back home.

About three o'clock on Sunday afternoon, Herman saw Bill on the street and asked if he had done any good.

"Oh, yeah," Bill said, "we got the truck and the driver is in jail."

Edwards was surprised. "What's the driver doing in jail?" he asked.

"Well, we got after him and had to run him all the way

to the top of the Smoky Mountains," Bill said, "and just before he crossed into Tennessee he still wouldn't stop, so we shot his tires out, took the truck, and put him in jail."

"What's he charged with?" Herman wanted to know.

"He was a-speedin', " Bill said.

The following day, Herman got a telephone call from the legal counsel of the *Knoxville Journal*.

The driver of the truck got out of jail.

And Bill Wright got his sixty dollars.

Lightning Struck Twice

Early in the 1960s when Thad Bryson was solicitor of the Thirtieth Judicial District, a woman came to his home one night and told him she wanted to swear out a warrant against a certain young man for rape.

Since the felony of rape was punishable at that time by death, Thad wanted to get all the information he could before issuing such a warrant. He took the woman into his office and asked her to tell him in detail what had happened.

She related that she had consented to go to a motion picture with the young man in Bryson City, and as soon as the picture show was over and they were outside, he suggested they walk to the rear of the theater where there was a narrow, dark alley.

"When we got to the darkest part back there," she said, "he grabbed me by the shoulders, threw me to the ground, tore off my clothes, and raped me."

"What resistance did you offer?" Thad asked.

"Oh, I didn't resist him," she said. "He's twice my size, and I was in fear of my life."

That made sense to Thad, but out of an abundance of caution he asked if there was anything else he should know.

"Yes," she said, "there is something else I think I should tell you. About ten days after he raped me, I met him on the street one afternoon, and he asked me if I would like to go to the show with him again. I said yes, and agreed to meet him at seven o'clock for the early show.

"We sat through the picture," she said, "and after the show when we walked outside, he suggested that we walk around behind the theater again.

"We did, and Mr. Bryson, when we came to the same spot where he had raped me before, darned if he didn't grab me again, throw me down, tear off my clothes, and rape me again!"

That was the end of the rape case. Thad didn't even ask if she went to the picture show with him a third time.

Magnanimity

The late Sam Queen, brother of the fiery Solicitor John M. Queen, lived in Maggie Valley in Haywood County. He was known far and wide as the dancingest man in the mountains. He was king of the cloggers, and he and his clog-dancing team had danced both for the president of the United States and the Queen of England.

Besides being a large landowner and operator of "Queen's Farm," a boardinghouse with riding horses and recreation facilities for tourists, Sam was also a professional bondsman. For an appropriate fee, he bonded people out of jail.

Living near the Cherokee Indian Reservation, Sam

formed a bond with the Indian people, and when an Indian got in trouble and was jailed in Haywood, Jackson, or Swain counties, he would usually call for Sam Queen to make his bond. When he bonded an Indian out of jail who had no place to go, Sam took him to Queen's Farm, generously letting him stay until his court trial.

He bonded a young Indian man one night and took him to the farm, gave him a bed, and put him up for two weeks. About a week before the young man's trial, in the middle of a night, the Indian stole into Sam's bedroom, took Sam's pistol, and shot Sam in his sleep. With murder on his hands, the young man fled in Sam's own car.

When he was captured, I placed him on my trial calendar for the felony of murder in the first degree with full intention of asking for the death penalty.

The week before our term of court was scheduled, I received a letter from the family of Sam Queen, signed by the widow and all of the children, saying in essence that they all knew of the love Sam had for the Cherokee Indian people, and that they knew that if Sam were alive he would not want the death penalty imposed in this case.

The Queen family asked me as solicitor to accept a plea of guilty to the felony of murder in the second degree and permit the Indian to receive a prison sentence in lieu of the death penalty.

The young man is now serving his sentence in the North Carolina Department of Corrections. In all my years as solicitor, I have never seen as magnanimous a gesture on the part of the family of a murder victim.

Your Driver's License, Please

A certain fellow was chief of police of a North Carolina mountain town for more than twenty years. He moved to Asheville when he retired, but kept his home in his hometown. He and his family commuted almost every weekend.

Coming home one Friday afternoon, he came upon a highway patrol check line where officers were examining every motorist's driver's license and registration card.

He showed his registration card, but had no driver's license. He had been driving since licenses were first required, and throughout his twenty years on the police force had never had nor had ever applied for a driver's license.

Busted Bile!

Frank Allen, former sheriff of Jackson County, was a good, efficient, and dedicated law enforcement officer, but he had one weakness: Every time he sat down, other than at his desk where he had something to do, he would fall asleep.

Once, during a superior court session in Sylva, Allen left the courtroom earlier than usual before the lunch break, made his way down to his office, sat down in a chair and leaned it back against the window, and as the sun streamed in on him, he went into a trance-like sleep, his head on the window ledge and his mouth gaped open so wide you could see his tonsils.

At twelve-thirty, Judge Hugh "Scotty" Campbell adjourned court for lunch, and he, Solicitor Thad Bryson,

Highway Patrolman Hayden Ferguson, Sheriff's Deputy Warfield Turpin, and I went to lunch. As we passed by the sheriff's office, I saw the sheriff asleep and called to the others to see the sleeping beauty.

Thad's sometimes perverted sense of humor came to the fore. "I wish we had a box of snuff," he said. "I'd like to see what would happen if we dropped some in his mouth."

Warfield, a great snuff lover, produced an unopened tin box of Bruton Snuff from his pocket, opened the lid, and stuck a kitchen match in it to get it good and loose. He handed it to Ferguson, who tiptoed to the sheriff, tipped the box over his gaping mouth, and tapped the bottom of the can.

The snuff broke loose, and the entire contents of the can dumped into Frank's mouth!

Beating a hasty retreat from the office, we all hid around the corner and waited for the reaction.

Suddenly we heard what sounded like a gunshot, but was just the front legs of Frank's chair banging to the floor—and out came Frank at a dead run, blowing brown puffs of snuff, juice running down his uniform.

He spied us in the corner, and trying to shout, he wheezed: "My God, boys, call the ambulance! Damned if I don't think my bile's busted!"

Running Gunfight

Sheriff Allen had a Chevrolet automobile he used in his job. It was an old model on which the license plate fitted in a bracket just under the right rear fender and projected several inches from the fender.

Both the sheriff and Highway Patrolman Hayden Ferguson prided themselves on being experts with their .38 Smith & Wesson revolvers. Late one afternoon the two decided to drive to Cashiers, the sheriff's home, and get in a little target practice.

Frank parked his car on the shoulder of a little-used road and set up a target to the right of the rear of the car. During the better part of twenty minutes they each shot about fifty rounds.

Oddly enough, when they checked the target, Ferguson had scored only four or five hits. The sheriff didn't realize that, by design, Ferguson had purposely missed the target—and had shot Allen's license plate full of holes, literally riddling it.

The next day, someone commented to Frank about his license plate, and the sheriff went out to inspect it.

He knew immediately what had happened—but wasn't about to admit Ferguson had pulled one on him.

He told his deputies the darnedest tale about a running gunfight with a bunch of South Carolina desperadoes who almost did him in and then got away. To add credence to his wild tale, in the presence of his deputies he even called the Walhalla, South Carolina, police department, and described the car and the desperadoes.

He turned the tables effectively: Ferguson never did mention the incident to Allen.

Sage Advice

A young highway patrolman, new on the force and relatively unfamiliar with the conduct and language of drunks, stopped a car and charged a highly intoxicated driver with driving under the influence.

On the way to jail, the drunk called the officer a son of a bitch several times.

At the jail, the officer saw his sergeant and called him to one side. He told him of the abusive language and what the drunk had called him.

Unperturbed, the sergeant said, "Son, to defendants, I became an immediate son of a bitch the day I was sworn in thirty years ago."

Slip of the Lip

One of the most brutal murders I have heard of here in the mountains was the bludgeoning of an elderly Haywood County man in an abandoned house in the "Frog Level" community.

But for an idle boast—actually a slip of the lip—the murderer might have remained free forever.

The old man who became the victim of this heinous crime lived in a rest home about a quarter of a mile from Frog Level. He had an unabashed love for Mogen David wine, and on the third day of each month, when his Social Security check arrived in the mail, he paid his fare at the rest home and saved about twenty-five dollars of the check.

He had only a short walk to Frog Level where he purchased his Mogen David, and then he proceeded faithfully to the abandoned house where he would drink himself out of his mind.

Knowing that the abandoned house was a haven for winos, the Waynesville chief of police had his officers check it every day, and on the fourth day of each month they always had to drag several drunks out, including the aforementioned old man.

One morning on the fourth day of the month, the officers who stopped by to check out the abandoned house found the man's body. He had been bludgeoned to death.

The only clue the officers had to work with was the fact that someone had seen a certain young man walking from the house about daylight that morning.

The young man was picked up by police and questioned at length, but he denied any knowledge of the murder. Since I did not have sufficient information on which to issue an indictment, the young man was released.

Through the next six months, officers worked diligently on the case of the old man's murder, but could turn up no further clue.

About eight months after the murder, the young man under suspicion was arrested for being publicly drunk. He was placed in the Haywood County jail in a cell with a man charged with breaking and entering and larceny.

The window of their cell overlooked the abandoned house in which the old man's murder had taken place.

The fellow prisoner asked the young man what he was charged with.

"I'm here for being drunk in town," the young man said, "but I'll be out and gone in about four hours. What'd they get you for?"

"Breaking and entering and larceny," the other said.

"Hell," the young man said, "we ain't got much to worry about. Look at that old house over there." He nodded out the window toward the abandoned house. "I beat the hell out of an old man over there with a two-by-four about six months ago, but they ain't got no proof on me. Breaking and entering ain't nothing. If they knew for sure I killed that old man I'd get the gas chamber."

To the young man, breaking and entering and larceny might have been "nothing," but to the man who was accused of those crimes, they were enough to put him away for a while. So the next time he talked to his attorney, he told him what the young man had told him.

The attorney came to me, asking some help for his client in return for his client's testimony against the young man. I quickly accepted the bargaining offer. I was ready and willing to make a deal if it gave us a break in the murder case.

I had the prisoner who was ready to sing tell his story to the officers who had been investigating the murder case. When he told them that the young man said he beat the old man to death with a two-by-four, the officers knew they had their man.

Good officers that they were, they had reported only that the old man had been beaten to death. They had not mentioned to anyone that the murder weapon had been a two-by-four.

I brought the young man to trial for first-degree murder. He was convicted and sentenced to die in the gas chamber.

Before the young man's execution date, the Supreme Court of the United States ruled that North Carolina's death penalty was unconstitutional, and the young man was returned to Haywood County and resentenced to serve the remainder of his natural life in prison.

He now serves his time.

The Best-Laid Plans

The best-laid plans often go awry . . . .

Two young Asheville men planned a burglary. They planned everything to the nth degree. They cased a house for a couple of weeks, charted the arrivals and departures of the family until a pattern developed, made a few dry runs, and then declared themselves ready for the event.

They drove by the house a couple of times, satisfied themselves that things were right, then parked in front of the house and broke in. For the next few minutes they carried loot from the house and piled it in the back of the car.

When they had enough they hopped in the car for their getaway—and the car wouldn't start. It was out of gas!

"Let's push it," one said. "We gotta get away from here."

They bailed out and pushed the car down the street.

A police cruiser came toward them, stopped, and the officer inquired, "What's going on?"

"Outta gas," one of the young men said nonchalantly. "We're pushing it to the station."

"Well, you're pushing it the wrong way on a one-way street," the officer said. He got out of his cruiser to write a ticket, saw the back seat filled with loot, and ran the young men in for breaking and entering.

Yes, the best-laid plans . . . .

Come and Get It

For more than twenty years, Warfield Turpin was deputy sheriff and jailor in Jackson County. His wife, Lillie, lived with him in the jail, and she was matron and cook.

In the 1950s Nantahala Power and Light Company commenced construction of a large hydroelectric plant, complete with dam, in the Glenville area, about thirty miles from Sylva.

Importing construction workers from all over the United States, Nantahala worked them hard for five days, and on Saturday they would come to Sylva to drink beer and raise hell.

As a consequence, every Sunday morning Lillie would wake up to a "drunk tank" full of men—sometimes seventy-five of them—all sick as dogs and with heads the size of big barrels.

For breakfast, Lillie would fill a large zinc washtub with eight or ten half-gallons of sauerkraut, stick it full of plastic spoons, shove it into the holding cell, and yell, "Come and get it!"

Those sick enough not to know better managed to stoke a few bites, but mostly they just stayed liquor-sick.

About midmorning, the superintendent of the job would come to the jail and bail out his men—and for that breakfast they each paid a five-dollar "jail board bill."

6 • *Movers and Shakers?*

Honors for the Day

During the 1959 session of the North Carolina General Assembly, John Kerr represented Warren County, a small county near the Virginia border. In 1941 John had been Speaker of the House of Representatives, and eighteen years later, there he was back as a new member of the House.

He was the son of Congressman John Kerr, for whom Kerr Reservoir was named. He was a great friend of mine and one of the most brilliant men I have ever known and undoubtedly the most eloquent speaker ever in the General Assembly.

During that session of the legislature, all the Democratic members of the House and Senate stayed at the Sir Walter Hotel on Fayetteville Street just below the capitol. The four lonesome Republicans stayed at the Andrew Johnson Hotel, about two blocks away.

The *Raleigh News & Observer*'s morning edition hit the streets about eleven-thirty on the night before, and a newsboy brought a bundle of papers to the lobby of the Sir Walter. Almost every day, the *News & Observer* would pick out a couple of representatives or senators and give them hell for one thing or another.

Most of the legislators would gather in the lobby about eleven-fifteen and wait for the morning edition of "Old Reliable" to see who got chosen that day.

One evening when we slowly gathered in the lobby of the hotel to wait the arrival of the paper, I looked up the marble steps to the mezzanine and saw John Kerr sitting up there by himself looking at the latest edition of *Time* magazine which that week featured President Eisenhower as "Man of the Year."

I went up the steps, sat down beside John, put my arm around his shoulders and asked, "Uncle John, what are you doing?"

He showed me Eisenhower's picture in the magazine, and said, "I'm a-sittin' here a-lookin' at the 'man of the year,' awaitin' up to see if I'm the 'son of a bitch of the day'. "

Speaker of the House

I dreamed the other night that Liston Ramsey, the Speaker of the North Carolina House of Representatives, died. When he reached the Pearly Gates, he introduced himself to St. Peter and asked if he might come in.

"Just a moment," St. Peter said. "Let me check." He thumbed through a thick book, studied a page a moment, and then said to Liston: "Yes, your name is here. However, there have been a few things in your life for which you will have to pay. You will be required to do penance for one year."

Liston thought that sounded fair. He asked what the penance was.

St. Peter beckoned toward a nearby fog bank, and from it came the ugliest, scrawniest, dirtiest, stinkingest, little old lady he had ever seen.

"Your penance," St. Peter said, gagging at the sight of the woman, "is that for one year you must remain hand-cuffed to this woman twenty-four hours a day."

Reluctantly, Liston agreed. If that was the only way, he was game.

About that time, Liston saw Jimmy Green, the lieuten-ant governor of North Carolina, walking down a broad red carpet, handcuffed to a beautiful buxom blonde made in the mold of Dolly Parton.

"Wait a minute," Liston said. "How come I have to do penance with this old crow and Jimmy Green is hand-cuffed to that lovely creature?"

"I'm afraid you don't understand," said St. Peter. *"She's the one who's doing penance."*

The Liquor Lobby

In the 1959 session of the North Carolina legislature, W. W. "Fat" Wall, who represented McDowell County, Leonard W. Lloyd, representative of Graham County, Lester Chalmers, solicitor of Wake County, and I formed a group that would have been referred to in mountain vernacular as "bosom buddies." We ran around together and shared a great many of the same enjoyments.

It was customary for us to leave Raleigh and go to our respective homes on weekends, returning for the Monday night session of the legislature which normally convened at eight o'clock and began our work week.

The liquor lobby was headed by a fine individual and able attorney from Charlotte, Frank Sims, a most persuasive lobbyist. Each week he would sack up two pints of the cheapest bourbon that could ever be made and have the bell boys deliver these brown paper pokes to the rooms of those representatives and senators who imbibed either occasionally or more than occasionally.

Each bag had in bold print on its side the room number to which it was to be delivered and it was placed upon the bed so that when we arrived on Monday night before the session, we could wet our whistles a bit.

Somehow the *Raleigh News & Observer* got wind of the system and sent a reporter on Tuesday to the room where the trash was dumped from the hotel each day. He collected all of the brown paper bags with the room numbers, and on Wednesday morning the entire center section of the *News & Observer* contained nothing but photographs of the empty paper bags with the room numbers showing, and the names of the representatives and senators who resided in those rooms printed under each picture.

Looking back, I must say that was a very effective journalistic presentation: Leonard, Fat, and I, all of whom came from "dry" counties, thought we were ruined.

That Wednesday afternoon, I called my friend, Les, and he, of course, had also seen the pictures. The four of us decided before anything else came up or anybody tried to interview us that we'd get out of Raleigh and go down to the coast for the rest of the week, hoping that by the weekend things would have blown over. We all met in the Sir Walter Hotel, got in my car, and headed for Currituck on the coast.

We stopped in Wilson, about fifty miles out of Raleigh, and bought plenty of good liquor to take along with us. We had a cooler with cold chasers, and some paper cups, and as we tooled along, with Fat driving, we sipped from our refreshments.

Fat decided he would take some of the secondary roads, thinking he could make better time and shorten the distance. He drove down a little road for several miles and came to an elevated drawbridge. On both sides of the creek, railings extended from the bridge for a distance up the road.

We crossed the bridge and continued on, and in about five minutes we came to another bridge, which looked exactly like the first. We crossed this one, too, and kept going. In another five minutes, we approached a third identical bridge.

"Fat," I said, "stop the car a minute."

He stopped and I got out and set my paper cup on the bridge, anchoring it with a rock. I thought the bridge looked powerful familiar—too familiar, actually.

Sure enough, five minutes later, we came to the fourth bridge—and on it sat my paper cup.

We had gone in circles at least three times!

When we finally got straightened out, we went on to Currituck without further incident and took rooms at an old farmhouse on the sound. The old man and his son who ran the boardinghouse were also fishing guides.

We stayed around till the weekend and were having such a good time that we decided to stay through the weekend and go back to Raleigh on Monday. Surely, we thought, by that time the liquor story would be blown over.

That weekend we decided to split up and do some team

fishing. Les and I went with the son in his boat in one direction, and Fat and Leonard and the old man went in another boat in the opposite direction. The team that brought home the most fish would win a bet.

We fished for a while, and Les and I hadn't caught a thing. We were bellyaching that we were going to lose the bet and finally the guide couldn't stand our complaining any longer.

"If fish is all you want," he said, "by golly, that ain't going to be no trouble. We can get you some fish—lots of 'em."

He pulled into a little cove where he had a trotline stretched across the water. As he began pulling in that line and taking off the bass, our eyes got bigger and bigger. When he finished, that stringer looked like a stalk of bananas. There must've been twenty huge bass on it.

When we pulled into the dock, Leonard was standing on the dock holding up a stringer with three little bass that looked like minnows. They weighed about a pound apiece.

When Les and I—it took both of us to lift the fish—pulled up that stringer and showed those twenty huge bass to Leonard, he almost fell off the dock.

Les and I collected the bet, and nobody said anything about how we caught the fish. There hadn't been any agreement on that. The bet had been on who brought home the most fish.

And when we got back to Raleigh, things were back to normal. Hardly anybody mentioned the *News & Observer* story.

Too many members of the legislature had been nailed by it, but I don't know of anybody else who left town because of it—or of anybody who had a better time that week.

Artistically Speaking

During the 1959 session of the North Carolina General Assembly, the Mellon Foundation offered to the state an art collection valued at six to eight million dollars. The only string attached was that North Carolina erect a suitable building in which the art collection would be housed.

John Kerr, one of the leaders of the House, was opposed to such an appropriation—roughly a million dollars—feeling that the money could be better spent on other projects.

As soon as the appropriations bill was introduced, Kerr announced his opposition. The following weekend, he went to his home in Warren County, and his wife and a group of her lady friends spent several hours with him, effectively arguing that man cannot live by bread alone and that North Carolina ought to take advantage of the Mellon Foundation's generous offer.

Apparently the womenfolk struck a chord in John, for he came back to Raleigh in favor of the appropriations bill. However, he told no one of his reversal of opinion.

The following day when the bill came up for consideration before the House, several representatives spoke in favor of the bill, and when John Kerr rose and sought recognition to speak, the rest of the House fully expected John's eloquence to kill the bill outright.

To their utter amazement, Kerr made a one-hour speech on why the appropriations bill should be adopted. In three sessions of the General Assembly, I had never heard as eloquent a speech.

As a result, North Carolina now has one of the few state-owned art museums in the United States.

The Very First

Liston Ramsey, Speaker of the North Carolina House of Representatives, has a large repertoire of amusing stories, such as this one:

A few years ago, the Pope passed away and went through the Pearly Gates to receive his just reward. St. Peter met him at the portal and welcomed him most effusively. He then escorted the Pontiff to a rather sparse room, approximately eight feet wide by ten feet, furnished only with a cot, a wash basin on a stand, and a slop jar on the floor.

Having been a frugal man on earth, the Pope gave no thought to the quality of the accommodations provided for him—until he strolled down the hall the next morning, and peering through an open doorway, saw a large and commodious sitting room with color television, a huge stereo, a large bedroom off the living room, and a bath made of the most beautiful marble with a walk down into the tub. The furnishings in the apartment were quite lavish.

A bit upset over the elaborate accommodations furnished to someone else, the Pope looked up St. Peter and complained of "the austerity of the room provided one who had been the reigning pontiff on earth for many years."

"Oh," St. Peter said. "You saw the other quarters."

"Yes," said the Pope, "as a matter of fact, I did."

"I can explain," said St. Peter. "You see, Your Eminence, that other apartment was given to an attorney who died a few weeks ago."

"An attorney!" said the Pope. "A lawyer? I fail to understand the difference in his quarters and those of a pope."

"Well, it's this way," St. Peter explained. "We have a couple of hundred popes up here—but this is the first lawyer we've been privileged to have!"

Automobile Tax

The late W. W. Wall of Marion served three sessions in the legislature with me. He was a self-made millionaire through dealing in scrap metal and junk. With little formal education, he had more native sense and good judgment than most.

Known by his friends as "Fat," he and I took week about driving to Raleigh, and once he said to me, "Buck, we ought to buy us a cheap little car to leave in Raleigh so both of us would have something to drive during the week."

I noticed in the paper the advertisement for a used car auction just outside of Raleigh every Wednesday. "I'll bet we could pick up a car cheap there," I told Fat.

That Wednesday, he found time to go to the auction, and when he inquired about purchasing a car the auctioneer rather rudely told him that only dealers could bid. Fat got mad and told me he was going to do something about the thing.

Researching, he found an obscure law on the books taxing a mule auction ten dollars for each mule sold. Fat went to the attorney general's office and had an amendment drawn to the "mule tax act" adding the words "and automobile auctions."

The next day, without an advance word to anyone, Fat rose on the floor of the House of Representatives and introduced his bill.

At first, there was little fanfare—but word got around

that evening, and the next morning all the lobbyists for the automobile industry throughout the state descended on Fat on bended knees, begging him to withdraw his bill.

In no uncertain terms and with the bark on, Fat told them of his experience at the auction. The lobbyists left, and Fat laughed up his sleeve.

Within the hour, the auctioneer, who only a couple of days before wouldn't give Fat the time of day, came into the hall of the House, put his arm around Fat's shoulders, and told him, "Come on down to the lot, old buddy, and pick out the car you want. You can have it for half the sale price."

So Fat got his car—but, honest man that he was, he paid the full price.

Then he withdrew his little bill.

7 • A Relative Matter

It All Started When . . .

In 1928 when I was five years old, my father, who ran a garage and gasoline station in Sylva, went to superior court to serve on the jury. Presiding at that session was the late, great Judge Felix E. Alley, Sr., of Waynesville. Judge Alley's wife, Elvira Hayes prior to her marriage, was related to me on the Leatherwood side through my paternal grandmother.

Thinking that court would be of some interest to me, and also to get me out from under my mother's feet for the day, my father took me with him to the courthouse and reported for jury duty.

Before the session began, he took me into the judge's chambers and introduced me to Judge Alley and explained the relationship between my grandmother and Judge Alley's wife.

At that time, Judge Alley was in his sixties, and was one of the most respected jurists that Western North Carolina had ever produced. He told my father that before they went into any jury trials he intended to take fifteen or twenty guilty pleas, and asked if it would be all right for me to come up to the bench and sit in a chair next to him. He said he would explain to me something of the workings of the court.

Several things made impressions on me. I remember vividly the brass spittoons scattered around the courtroom. Everybody—judge, jury, and spectators—chewed tobacco. A spittoon sat on the floor between the judge and me, and he occasionally lowered his head and spat into it.

Defendants came one by one to stand before the bench of justice, some with lawyers, some without. The defendant would enter his plea, the investigating officer would testify what his investigation had disclosed—and the hard facts of life unfolded there at the judge's bench. It was a most fascinating experience for a boy of five.

I determined then and there that I would become a lawyer, and I cannot recall any instance or occasion that deterred me from the resolve made that day in Jackson County Superior Court through the kind auspices of Judge Felix E. Alley, Sr.

Big Doc's Cure

"Big Doc" Nichols was for many years the family doctor of the Buchanan clan. We went to him for everything from tonsillectomies to circumcisions.

Once, around the age of five or six, when I caught a terrible cold, my father took me to Big Doc. I had been running a high fever, couldn't go to school, and had driven my parents crazy.

My father and I walked into the drugstore in Sylva where Big Doc held forth on a big leather couch in the rear of the building.

"Big Doc," my father said, "Little Buck's had a cold for a week, and nothing we give him has helped him a'tall. What about looking at him and seeing what you can do for him?"

Big Doc leaned his four hundred pounds a little deeper into the sofa, put his hands behind his head, and said to my father, "Buck, they ain't nobody can cure the cold, but I'll tell you what: Let him run around outside in the cold without many clothes on till he catches pneumonia. I want you to know right now, I'm hell on curing pneumonia."

The Neighborly Way

Soon after Harry and Pearl Buchanan moved from Sylva to Hendersonville in the 1930s, Aunt Pearl hired a country girl named Dessie, about eighteen years old, to help around the house.

There were no dial telephones then; all calls had to be placed through "Central." Hendersonville was a small town in which everybody knew everyone else's business, and if you picked up the phone to call a number, you could just tell "Central" the name of the party you wanted and the operator would plug you in.

At first, Dessie was afraid of the telephone. She had never spoken on one. But Aunt Pearl finally familiarized her with answering the gadget. She still hadn't taught her to place a call, but Dessie could answer the contraption all right.

One afternoon Aunt Pearl was busy preparing for her bridge club and realized she needed a dozen eggs and a pound of butter. Too busy in the kitchen to call for the things she needed, Aunt Pearl told Dessie to pick up the phone, and ask for the A&P, and tell whoever answered to deliver her a pound of butter and a dozen eggs.

With some reluctance, Dessie undertook the task. She put the phone to her ear, and when Central answered, Dessie asked her to please ring the A&P.

"I am sorry," Central said. "That line is busy."

"Well, when they ain't so busy," Dessie said, "tell 'em to send Mrs. Buchanan a dozen eggs and a pound of butter right quick."

A half-hour later, the delivery was made.

Change of Plans

Around 1936, my father built the family a small brick home in the sleepy little town of Webster. He hired Uncle George Hoxit, one of the last good rock masons in the area, to build a chimney and fireplace out of native stone picked up in the area around the house.

Uncle George was in his mid-seventies, about five-feet-five, and bald-headed. He had a quick wit.

One afternoon when the job was almost finished, I went with Dad to see how it looked. Uncle George was up on the scaffolding finishing the top of the chimney, and Dad and I stood just in front watching him apply the finishing touches.

Suddenly, because of some unnoticed imbalance, the chimney began to move, and it was obvious it was going to fall.

Uncle George jumped to the ground, and in a calm, totally unexcited voice, turned to Dad and said, "Mr. Buck, look out—I'm changing my plans!"

New Orleans or Bust!

I was in law school at the University of North Carolina at Chapel Hill in 1948 when Charlie "Choo Choo" Justice led the Tar Heel football team into the Sugar Bowl in New Orleans against Charlie Trippi and the University of Georgia.

Jane and I lived in Victory Village, a barracks-type housing unit for veterans of World War II. I went to school under the G.I. Bill of Rights and Jane worked to supplement our income. A young man from Elkin named Jim Taylor lived next door to us, and he too was going to school on a shoestring.

One day in class, Jim and I were seated in front of Melville Broughton, Jr., son of the former governor and senator from North Carolina, who told us that he planned to go to the Sugar Bowl on the Carolina Special, a train that ran from Chapel Hill to New Orleans and carried Carolina fans to the game.

Jim and I wanted to go to the game but neither of us had the money to go either by car or by special train. Somehow that day, during all the talk about the Sugar Bowl, we managed to make a bet with Mel Broughton that we could make the trip to New Orleans on ten dollars, exclusive of the student ticket for the game, which we could buy in Chapel Hill. Mel wagered each of us fifty dollars to our ten dollars we could not make the trip for that amount.

We left Chapel Hill with a ten-dollar bill and what we would need in a traveling bag, determined to hitch-hike to New Orleans. Neither of us knew enough about geography to know that it was 1,100 miles to New Orleans—one way.

We thumbed rides in the worst of weather. It rained, sleeted, and snowed on us most of the way. We stopped in Biloxi, Mississippi, and divided a can of sardines and a nickel box of crackers for lunch one day. We slept in bus stations and napped under any cover we could find.

Finally, on the morning of the game, we arrived in New Orleans. We must have looked like two bums sitting in the Carolina section, and we had the opportunity to shake hands with Mel Broughton, just to let him know we made it to the game.

My uncle, Harry E. Buchanan of Hendersonville, had come to the game on the Carolina Special and was staying at the Roosevelt Hotel in the heart of the city. After the game (which Georgia won, incidentally), Jim and I went up to Uncle Harry's suite in the Roosevelt.

Finding our plight to be severe—we had only four dollars and fifteen cents between us—Uncle Harry offered to provide us with a room for the night, but of course our wager precluded that. The wager, however, said nothing about where we mooched meals, so we let my uncle order up two of the finest meals either of us had ever seen. We gulped the food down like two hungry wolves.

In late evening, we started hitch-hiking for home. We straggled back into Chapel Hill with two-day growths of beard, we were almost frozen to death, and we would have cheerfully eaten sole leather had it been available.

It took our wives a week to get us filled up and back to normal—and when we went back to class following the New Year's break, we didn't hesitate to accept the two crisp fifty-dollar bills handed to us by Mel Broughton.

Mister Mayor

In 1943 I married into one of the finest families anywhere. My father-in-law, the late Roscoe Poteet, although an uneducated man in terms of formal learning, started work with the Mead Corporation in Sylva in his teens and retired as general superintendent of the Sylva Division several years before his death in 1980.

Not only was he an inspiration to me, but his sage advice along with his exceptional intelligence and his practical sense, was always available when I needed it—and, frankly, I needed it often.

In the 1950s when there were no legal liquor stores in the area and those of us who drank occasionally had to procure our spirits from the local moonshiners, Roscoe traded with a fine old man in the Canada section of Jackson County, a remote, rural area that the sheriff left pretty well alone.

Roscoe was the lone Democratic member of the Board of Aldermen of the Town of Sylva and had just announced that he was running for mayor in the election coming up in about three months. He announced as a Democrat against the Republican opponent, the late Hugh Monteith, a local lawyer—and the politics began to heat up.

Sylva then had a force of two policemen, Penny Bryson and a big, fat officer whose name I do not recall. For the sake of this story, let's call him Big John.

On a Friday afternoon shortly before the election, Roscoe drove his green Oldsmobile to his supplier in the Canada Township and procured two half-gallons of the finest corn liquor, put them in the trunk of his car, and covered them with a piece of old felt where they would not be seen without being uncovered. He then drove the twenty-odd miles back to Sylva to his home with eager anticipation of sampling the stuff.

As he drove through Sylva, however, he noticed his car was low on gasoline, so he pulled into Grayson Cope's service station and told Grayson to "fill 'er up."

Suddenly the lone Sylva police car pulled in beside him and Penny Bryson got out and walked to the window of Roscoe's car. "I'm sorry, Mr. Poteet," he said, "but we have had a report that a green Oldsmobile was headed toward Sylva with a load of white liquor, and your car matches the description." Lowering his voice, he added, "I'm not going to search your car here, but John and I will follow you home and look."

He was clearly playing both ends against the middle because his job depended on the coming election. During those days we were not bound by all the ill-advised rules hampering towns from hiring and firing as they choose.

Roscoe drove home, about a half-mile away, and Penny and Big John followed. Penny called Roscoe to one side. "I know you've got some liquor in that trunk," he said, "but if it's covered up, we won't move anything to find it."

Roscoe opened the trunk, and Big John immediately flipped the felt, uncovering Roscoe's moonshine. John confiscated the whiskey and placed Roscoe under arrest.

However, lacking a search warrant and not having complied with other search procedures required by the law, the liquor could not be introduced into evidence and the case was dismissed.

Although Roscoe was acquitted, Big John turned one of the half-gallons over to a local taxi driver who parked on Main Street, and on the day before the election and on election day itself, the taxi driver prominently displayed the liquor to all who passed by, telling everyone where it came from and asking if they wanted to vote for a man like that.

Apparently they did: Roscoe was elected mayor by a wide margin.

As soon as the election returns were in and it was apparent that Roscoe had been elected mayor and all five Democratic aldermen had also been elected, Sheriff Griffin Middleton, an ardent Democrat in the Harry Truman mold, telephoned Penny Bryson.

"Penny," Griffin said, "I want to report that there's a green Oldsmobile with MAYOR Roscoe Poteet in it headed toward city hall with a load of five Democratic alderman!"

Before the following Monday morning when Roscoe and his board were sworn in, both Penny and Big John had resigned and turned in their gear.

Incidentally, Roscoe remained mayor for twenty-four years before he chose not to seek reelection. He was a great man who accomplished more, not only for himself but for others, than anyone else I've ever known.

The Chaser

My uncle, Carl Buchanan, and I used to go to my father-in-law's house, Roscoe Poteet's, almost every Saturday night to play poker with Roscoe and two or three of his cronies.

We always had corn squeezings in adequate quantities, and we drank it straight from juice glasses, chasing it with a glass of water from the faucet.

One Saturday night, Bill Wise, Roscoe's neighbor, had just poured himself a half juice glass of corn when he was called to the table to place his bet during a game of stud.

He sat his glass of corn on the sink.

Carl, having folded his hand, decided it was time for a drink, so he filled his glass half full of corn, walked over to the sink, and swallowed the 160-proof in one gulp.

Starting to turn on the faucet, he saw Bill's glass half full of what Carl thought was water, so he grabbed it and soaked it down, chasing corn with corn.

It took him thirty minutes to recover after turning on the faucet, putting his mouth under it, and drinking at least a half-gallon of water.

Tears streamed out of his eyes the rest of the night.

Piping It Up

In the 1950s when I was attorney for the Town of Sylva, the town was "dry" and the nearest place to purchase legal liquor was at the West Asheville ABC Store, some forty-five miles away. About half of that store's business came from the far western counties.

Realizing the revenue being lost by the town, the mayor and board of aldermen instructed me to get enabling legislation to hold a referendum on the establishment of an ABC store in Sylva.

Then as now, North Carolina had a uniform system of such stores. All liquor prices were and are uniform throughout the state; the stores were and are run by municipalities under local ABC boards appointed by the city fathers.

I drew up such a bill for presentation to the legislature but could not get any of the senators or representatives representing Jackson County to introduce the bill. They were afraid to do so for political reasons. After determining this, I went to them one by one and persuaded them to not oppose the measure, if I could get the bill introduced by some member of the legislature from elsewhere.

I felt that they thought I could not persuade any legislator not representing Jackson County to do so, but that year my uncle, Harry Buchanan, who had been mayor of Sylva before moving to Hendersonville, was elected to the state Senate, and he introduced the bill.

The measure was passed, the referendum held, and an ABC store began operating in Sylva within a few months.

Shortly after it opened, I decided to put an air conditioner in the window of my law offices on the second floor of the Professional Drug Building. In order to get a 220-volt wire to the conditioner, the electricians had to put a one-inch metal pipe up the exterior of the building and run the wire through that to protect it from the elements.

While the electricians were putting up the conduit, two old men, close friends of mine, were sitting on the stoop in front of the Sylva Supply Building across the street. They watched the operation for a while, then one remarked to the other, "I knew Little Buck was responsible for getting the liquor store, but damned if I knew they were going to pipe it up to him!"

The Aging Process

Uncle John Morris was an educated, articulate man—when he wanted to be—who ran the Sylva Insurance Agency. He had a camp in Whiteside Cove, a remote area in the south end of Jackson County, about thirty miles from Sylva, and like most of us he enjoyed a drop or two of corn squeezings occasionally.

My office in Sylva, one room heated by a wood stove, was next to Uncle John's upstairs in the Sylva Supply Building. Since Uncle John had been a lifelong friend of my family, we quickly formed a sort of father-son relationship which endured until his death.

One day we went out to his camp in Whiteside Cove and took with us two half-gallons of spirits, and that night, with the help of a few friends who dropped in, we consumed one of the half-gallons.

Next morning, fearing someone would break in and steal the other jar, Uncle John and I went up the hillside across the headwaters of the Chatuge River and buried it near a landmark we knew we could locate later.

A few months later, we returned to his camp to spend a night and immediately went across the river and tore up the hill to retrieve the moonshine. Unfortunately, we had lost the reference points. We knew the jar was there, we just couldn't find it.

Fearful of snakebite, we decided to return home that night, but we didn't give up. Every time we went to his camp after that, we spent a couple of hours digging up that hillside, looking for our lost tonic. Uncle John died, and I have looked since then.

The liquor has never been found. If there is any truth to the story that aging liquor improves it, I hope some good Democrat of the John Morris stripe is the one who finally finds our jug!

Sentimental Journey

In 1952, when I was chairman of the Democratic Committee of Jackson County, we planned to hold a political rally in Cashiers, and I was to secure the speaker. Immediately I thought of Judge Felix E. Alley, a distant relative whom I regarded highly.

Judge Alley had been born in Cashiers, and had walked the twenty-five miles from Cashiers to Cullowhee to get his education at Cullowhee Normal School, now Western Carolina University. He then went on to law school and became one of the most distinguished judges on the bench.

Now in his eighties and retired from the bench, he was known and loved throughout Cashiers—I knew that.

I called Judge Alley and he kindly agreed to speak at the seven o'clock rally if I would drive to Waynesville, pick him up, take him to the rally, and return him home afterward. I agreed to do that.

On the appointed day I drove him to Cashiers where we enjoyed a wonderful meal, and promptly at seven I introduced the judge to a group of more than three hundred of his lifelong friends.

He launched into one of those fiery Democratic speeches, giving them, in Harry Truman's words, pure hell. For thirty minutes he dwelt upon that subject, praising the Democratic Party and its principles.

Then he toned down his words into a sentimental talk to his friends, with whom he had grown up and gone to school. He began reminiscing, telling anecdotes of his youthful days in Cashiers. Time literally flew. No one looked at his watch. Each person sat on the edge of his seat, trancelike, soaking in every word by this old man in his golden years. Before anyone realized it, two hours and forty minutes had flown by without a single fidget in the audience.

When Judge Alley concluded, with tears streaming

down his craggy old face, he stepped from the podium; the audience rose in unison, and for ten minutes gave him a great ovation.

It was then another full hour before I could get him away. Every man, woman, and child shook his hand and bade him best wishes.

It was far, far past the old man's bedtime when we reached his home. He was tired but happy and exhilarated, for his audience's enthusiasm had attested not only to his remarkable eloquence but to the love that the people of Cashiers held for this great old judge.

Favorite Food

Squirrel is my favorite wild meat, especially when cooked in a pie with plenty of golden brown crust on top, lots of juice in the middle, and a pile of rice on the side—the way my wife Jane fixes it.

Several years ago a sheriff in a western county of my district came by my office and in the course of conversation mentioned that he had a half-dozen fat young squirrels in his freezer. After much persuasion, I talked him out of them. He said he was going to a party in Waynesville the next night and would drop the squirrels off for me on his way.

The next day around six o'clock he stopped by my home in Sylva and left a paper poke for me. Jane, knowing of the planned squirrel delivery, put the bag in the freezer.

Three or four days later the sheriff called to ask if I had eaten my squirrels. When I told him I had not, he suggested that I look at them before Jane got ready to cook.

When I opened the freezer and the paper bag, I found

therein two fifths of Wild Turkey, the sheriff's favorite brand of bourbon!

He had taken the wrong poke to the party, and during the happy hour proudly opened his brown bag and pulled out the frozen squirrels.

Since, however, this was before my ulcers decreed no more Wild Turkey for me, I can assure you that the sheriff did not receive a swap back, but later, bless his heart, I also got my squirrels.

That's an Order

Ethel Sutton, one of the grandest ladies I have known, has been my secretary for more years than either of us cares to admit, both while I practiced law and while I have been solicitor.

I call her "Auntie," a habit I fell into when my young son first called her that.

Throughout the years her great sense of humor has been expressed in the number of cartoons and drawings she clips and places on the outer door to the rest room in her office. Some of those cartoons are ribald, and all are funny.

Claude Sitton, a redheaded young man from Morganton, succeeded Sam Ervin as resident judge when Sam was appointed to the federal bench. When he came to Sylva to hold his first court, he saw Auntie's cartoons and laughed till tears ran down his cheeks.

They formed a close and lasting bond, and every morning before court and at every recess Judge Sitton would come into Auntie's office and read and chuckle and laugh aloud at the pictures and sayings pinned to her door.

Finally, at the noon recess on the last day of court, Judge Sitton came in and without a smile on his face, said to her: "Auntie, I'm going to lunch. You stay here and when I get back I want you to have all that low-down stuff off that door—and make me a Xerox copy of every one of them before you put 'em back!"

Good Question

When my son, Mark, was three years old, the doctor, after treating a lasting sore throat, recommended a tonsillectomy. Admitting him to the hospital, the doctor suggested that since he was going to have to put Mark to sleep anyway, he might just as well circumcise him at the same time.

His mother and I agreed, and the surgeon performed both operations.

When Mark awakened, he was in pain, but he had a wondering look on his face, also.

"Daddy," he asked, "where were my tonsils?"

"In your throat, son, but they're there no longer."

"If they were in my throat," he asked, "why do I hurt so bad down here?"

The I-Don't-Care Syndrome

Several years ago, an elderly man by the name of Jim Cahoon lived in Currituck County. His large, three-story white house sat partially on the sound. The rear porch and deck area were supported by pilings in the water.

Across the front of his house was a balcony on the

second floor with French doors entering a sitting room upstairs.

Jim's only occupation from his early childhood days was guiding fishermen and hunters on Currituck Sound, and he had made a good living at it.

In his later years, however, guiding became too strenuous and he and his wife established their home as a boardinghouse for tourists. They had wonderful meals and nice, comfortable rooms.

My wife, Jane, and I went down almost every summer for a week or ten days, and discovered that Jim had an affinity for drinking liquor somewhat to excess, a habit that pleased Mrs. Cahoon not one whit. She was always on his back about drinking.

In the summer of 1976, Jane and I went to Currituck for ten days of that wonderful Cahoon hospitality. We left home early one morning and drove the five hundred miles to Jim's home by early evening.

At our knock, Mrs. Cahoon admitted us into the large living room, and there sat Jim in a big easy chair with both legs and both arms in casts and a bandage around his bald head.

My first question, of course, was, "Jim, what in the world happened to you?"

Mrs. Cahoon spoke up quickly. "I can tell you what happened to him, Mr. Buchanan. About three months ago, we decided to remove the porch and balcony. We left the French doors where they were until we could have the place fixed like we wanted it.

"Last week, Jim got on one of his benders, forgot that we had taken off the porch and balcony, and walked through the French doors to get some fresh air.

"He went eighteen feet straight down and landed on

that concrete patio.

"That's why he's in the shape he's in today, Mr. Buchanan, and to be perfectly honest with you—I don't care!"

More Than Coffee

Once in the winter, with about a fifteen-inch snow on the ground, Frank Allen, Griff Middleton, Thad Bryson, several others and I, went to a remote section in Canada Township to camp at Rough Butt Bald. We had an ample supply of corn squeezings tucked into our jeep along with our gear.

Near a bold spring, Weaver Swangim had a tarpaper shack built in a little swale. There were enough bunks to bed us down, and a fifty-five gallon drum for a wood stove to keep us from freezing to death from the outside in; the corn juice took care of us from the inside out.

Weaver had a copper top from an old liquor still for a coffee pot. It held about three gallons. Upon arrival, Weaver built a fire in the drum, and in our customary manner put the coffee on by pouring two pounds of coffee in the still cap and filling it with three gallons of water.

We camped three nights, had plenty of corn, plenty of coffee, and a good time.

When we were ready to leave, I had the job of carrying the still cap out to a large rock and banging it hard enough on the rock to pop the coffee grounds out. They came out in one piece, and on top of what had been the bottom of the grounds in the still cap was a mother mouse and five tiny offspring.

Now, I have sort of a queasy stomach—but nothing to compare with the rest of that crowd. I hollered them out and showed them what I had found.

Someone hollered, "Have we not got a bit of liquor left?"

We hadn't—until Sheriff Middleton remembered he had a half-gallon of "evidence" in his jeep. It was to be used in a case coming up the next week.

Solicitor Bryson assured the sheriff that if he would let us drink the liquor he would take care of it in court—some way.

With that half-gallon, we drowned out the memory of those mice—and the next week when that half-gallon was introduced into evidence, thank goodness the defense counsel didn't ask to examine the contents: pure spring water.

Brevity Record

In April of 1982 I had the pleasure of speaking to the Law Day banquet of attorneys, secretaries, court officials, and judges at a luncheon meeting in Henderson County.

I was introduced by my good friend, Attorney Monroe Redden, Jr., who spent fifteen minutes on my introduction, and concluded by admonishing me to make my remarks very brief and very humorous.

I told the group that Monroe's introduction reminded me of a talk I once made to a Rotary Club. The club president spent forty-five minutes introducing me, and then brought me on by saying that I would "make a brief talk on sex."

I stood and said, "Gentlemen, it gives me great

pleasure," and sat back down.

8 • *Here, There, and Yonder*

Another One, Please

Before the decision of the North Carolina Supreme Court holding that an indigent person, although entitled to adequate representation, could not have the attorney of his choice, some judges followed the practice of permitting an indigent person the opportunity of making limited choices.

One day in Guilford County Superior Court, an accused person was brought in for arraignment. The presiding judge advised the man of his rights with respect to representation by a lawyer to be paid by the state. At that moment, it being time for the calendar call, the courtroom was filled with members of the defense bar.

Having completed his advice, the judge told the defendant that he could have the services of any lawyer in the courtroom. "Further," the judge said with mirth in his voice, "if you don't like the looks of these, I'll try to find one somewhere else."

The defendant examined carefully and deliberately the appearance and demeanor of every lawyer in the courtroom, turned to the judge, and said, "If Your Honor please, I will take anyone other than these."

Don't Antagonize Him!

A Morehead City attorney's religious life left everything to be desired. "Come to think of it," one of his acquaintances said, "his life left everything to be desired."

A local minister felt this attorney was a class-action test case for the ministry. Every effort to bring him around to even a semireligious posture failed.

Finally the lawyer's health failed, too—and in a big way. First, he was confined to his home, and later to the hospital.

When he felt the poor fellow had both feet in the grave, the minister gauged it time to launch his final assault.

He strode into the hospital room, looked at the shadow of a man lying in the bed, and exclaimed, "Renounce the Devil!"

The old attorney opened his eyes slightly and grimaced. "Preacher, don't push me," he uttered. "I ain't in condition to antagonize nobody!"

A Definite Problem

Harold Hoffman, court reporter for the Thirtieth Judicial District, decided to fly to London and visit relatives. He boarded a 747 at New York's John F. Kennedy International Airport and relaxed as the plane became airborne.

Harold had a window seat, and an hour or two after takeoff he was looking out the window when the captain came on the intercom and said, "Ladies and gentlemen, our number four engine—the one on the far right side— has quit functioning, but I want to assure you that this airplane was designed to fly beautifully on three engines. However, we will be approximately two hours late arriving in London."

Reassured, Harold leaned back in his seat and ordered a bourbon and water. In a few minutes, the captain came on again and said, "Ladies and gentlemen, our number one engine—the one on the far left side—has quit running, but do not be alarmed: This airplane was designed to run beautifully on two engines. The only problem is that we will now be four hours late arriving in London."

Harold noticed the rather plump woman seated beside him, an apparent veteran flyer, was not in the least concerned, and thus reassured, he settled down and ordered another bourbon and water.

Another half-hour passed, and the captain came on again and said, "Ladies and gentlemen, our number two engine has just quit, but I want to assure you that this airplane was designed to fly safely on only one engine. We will, however, now be delayed in arriving in London by about eight hours."

By that time, no one could reassure Harold. As sweat popped out on his brow, he turned to the plump lady beside him and shouted, "My God, I hope that other engine don't go or we'll never get down!"

Topsy-Turvy

Solicitor H. W. "Butch" Zimmerman, Jr., of Lexington, holding court in one of his smaller counties where court week still attracted a crowd, noticed an elderly gentleman day after day sitting on the second row of benches. As time passed the solicitor noticed also that the old man would spit tobacco juice on the floor and "rub it out" with the sole of his shoe, and occasionally would "break wind" without any embarrassment at all.

Zimmerman proceeded one morning to call the docket and arraign the various defendants. About midway through his calling of the docket, the old gentleman delivered one of his better "bench-splitters" which raised him halfway off the bench.

"The entire courtroom heard it," Butch said later, "and I am sure it vibrated the bench for its entire twenty feet."

The judge immediately inquired, "What, Mr. Solicitor, was that?"

"If Your Honor please," Zimmerman answered, "I believe the gentleman was just clearing his throat."

With a twinkle in his eye, the judge replied, "To be sure, Mr. Solicitor, if indeed he was, he is sitting on his face!"

The Judge's Pitcher

One of the "regular customers" of the Hertford County jail was serving a sentence in the capacity of "trustee" during a session of superior court.

The jail was adjacent to the courtroom, and Sheriff James E. Baker, who liked to keep iced water on the bench for the presiding judge, told the trustee, "Go to the court-room and get the judge's pitcher."

A few minutes later Sheriff Baker saw the trustee coming back with a large, expensive portrait of one of Hertford County's late judges which had been hanging in the courtroom just behind the judge's bench.

"What in the world are you doing with that painting?" the sheriff asked the trustee.

Nonplussed, the trustee replied, "You tol' me to get the judge's pitcher, and that's the onliest one I saw!"

Some Good in Most

A few years ago, Dr. John T. Bunn, pastor of First Baptist Church in Sylva, was requested to appear as a character witness in a trial in Lillington, North Carolina, a city of Harnett County on the banks of the Cape Fear River.

"This was one of those unusual cases," Dr. Bunn related, "in which the defendant actually had a character which could be testified to."

He was duly sworn in and after a few tributes to the good character of the defendant, the prosecutor took over.

"Now, Dr. Bunn," he questioned, "you are a minister, are you not?"

Although he wanted to deny it, Dr. Bunn figured the prosecutor had him dead to rights. "Yes," he replied.

"Then by training and profession," the prosecutor said, "you look for the best in people, do you not?"

Bunn pleaded guilty to that charge.

In an effort to drive his point home, the prosecutor said in a syrupy voice and with a smirk spread across his face, "Preacher, you can find some good in the worst person, can you not?—the guiltiest person, even a reprobate, can't you?"

That's when Dr. Bunn went into ministerial overdrive. "You'd better believe it," he shot back. "I can even find some good in most attorneys!"

Not Even Close

In the 1950s when Superior Court Judge E. Maurice Braswell was district solicitor in Cumberland County, the county managed to get one of the new breathalyzer machines for its highway patrolmen.

A week after the newspapers gave the new machine a lot of publicity, State Highway Patrolman Hargrove arrested a man on the Murchison Road for driving under the influence of intoxicating liquor.

On the way back to the courthouse, the subject of arrest kept muttering that he "wanted one of them scientific tests."

Finally Hargrove asked, "Just what kind of scientific test do you want?"

"You know," said the accused, "I want one of them autopsies."

The Shortest Ceremony

No judge ever had more redoubtable fame in Nash County than Judge Bantholomew. He was noted for brevity in all things other than sentences.

In one hand, the judge carried the club of righteousness, and in the other the staff of mercy. The problem was, he never let his right hand know what his left hand was doing. Yet, when the chips were down, old Judge Bantholomew always seemed to come through.

One balmy spring night, the judge was rousted from a fitful sleep by the incessant rattle of pebbles against his bedroom window. He rose from his bed like a hound of hell to declare the person outside "incompis mentis," which is the legal definition of a six-ply, nonskid, puncture-proof idiot.

To his great surprise, in a buggy on the lawn below was a young couple well known to the judge. Before he could open his mouth to castigate the young man for waking him in the middle of the night, the young man shouted, "Judge, either marry us quick or be a witness to murder. Her pa's a-coming up the road and we only got a two-minute head start."

With unequaled conciseness, Judge Bantholomew shouted, "Hitched! Now git!"

That holds the Nash County, Eastern North Carolina, and Baptist World Alliance record for the shortest wedding ceremony ever performed.

Assault with a What?

A criminal law class was discussing the difference between impossibility of fact to commit a crime and impossibility of law to commit a crime.

A case in question was that in which an impotent man was charged with attempted rape. The question was whether the man could be charged with attempted rape when he could not be charged with rape due to his impotence.

The professor asked a student with what crime the defendant was charged, and before the student could respond, someone in the back of the room blurted out, "assault with a dead weapon."

Where Could He Be?

Nestled in the bosom of the Old North State, only a few miles from Raleigh, is the old Wake Forest College campus. Once at the heart of the campus was the law school, which occupied the upper floor of the library building.

One of the deans of the law school felt the students held him in contempt. What he didn't know was that they were trying not to hold him in contempt. Prank after prank was perpetuated with malice aforethought against the dean.

On one occasion the students posted a notice on the door of the dean's office informing all of the dean's sudden death and departure. The note was worded this way: "Dean L. started for heaven today."

The next morning the death notice was replaced with the following: "Great consternation in heaven. Dean L. has not yet arrived!!!"

Charlie or Charlene?

Once when Jerry Townson was prosecuting the docket in Johnson County District Court, he called the name Charlie Smith. Out of the corner of his eye he saw that a large woman had come up.

He called Charlie Smith again. The woman just stood there. He looked over to see why and was amazed at the size of the woman.

She stood more than six feet tall, weighed about two hundred pounds, and had arms that reached almost to her knees. She was dressed in a skirt and white sweater.

Because of her size, she probably had difficulty finding a bra with straps long enough, so her bra cups rested rather high on her chest, giving her a "thrown back" look. She wore panty hose and no shoes, only ankle socks.

Townson was surprised to see a pronounced stubble on the woman's face; she had not shaved that day.

The judge leaned forward and asked of the woman, "Are you Charlie Smith?"

"Yes, sir," Charlie Smith squeaked in a falsetto voice.

The judge had no trouble ascertaining that Charlie was no woman; he suggested that Charlie leave the courtroom until he could get into some proper clothing.

Charlie later returned dressed in trousers and shirt. He was charged with larceny, having tried to shoplift some large-sized women's shoes and underwear. A clerk who saw him put a large pair of bikinis under his sweater and tried to detain him had been pushed over a counter for her efforts. A male assistant manager tried to block Charlie's dash for the door and got overrun for his trouble.

A policeman happened to be in the parking lot when Charlie ran out, and hearing the shouts from those in the store, the policeman gave chase.

Thinking he was chasing a woman, the officer was surprised that he had trouble gaining on her. He testified that he lunged and grabbed Charlie by the hair—and the hair came off Charlie's head. Startled by the wig, the officer paused momentarily, then gave chase again, and only with the greatest difficulty did he manage to run Charlie down.

After hearing the testimony, the judge sentenced Charlie to thirty days in jail.

Leaving the courtroom, the officer remarked to Townson that the only reason he had been able to catch up with Charlie was because of the tight skirt Charlie was wearing.

"He could only take short steps," the officer said, "about a foot at a time. It was amazing how fast his legs moved in that tight skirt. If he had thought to pull the skirt above his knees like women do when they're running, I never would have caught him."

Nolo Contendere

Chief District Judge Fentress Horner presided and Assistant Solicitor Tom Watts prosecuted that day in 1971 in Pasquotank County District Court. The courtroom was full, for the calendar was lengthy at the regular Thursday court session.

Solicitor Watts called the calendar and the defendants or their lawyers told the court and prosecutors what pleas they wanted to enter.

Halfway through the calendar call, Watts called the name of a defendant accused of a minor motor vehicle violation. Herbert Mullen, a Pasquotank lawyer, unfolded his lanky frame from a chair and stated, "Your Honor, my client will enter a plea of nolo contendere."

The judge and the solicitor said the plea would be acceptable to them. Nolo contendere is defined as a refusal by the defendant to contest the validity of the charge, which allows the court to impose punishment.

Watts next called a fellow named Jasper, a frequent guest of the Pasquotank County court and jail, who faced his usual charge of public drunkenness from the previous weekend.

Jasper customarily sat upon the back bench, the most

convenient place from which to slip out in the corridor to imbibe in some bottled courage. He had apparently just returned from restoring his nerve, for when Watts roared, "Jasper, how do you plead?" Jasper bolted upright and exclaimed, "Judge, Yer Honor, I think I'll do one of them nolo things, too."

Judge Horner frowned at the chuckles from the audience and inquired, "Sir, do you know the meaning of a plea of nolo contendere?"

"I sure do, Judge," Jasper replied. "That's a gentleman's way of pleading guilty."

Bale of Cotton

Years ago in Eastern North Carolina there lived an extremely colorful judge who actively held a superior court bench into his mid-eighties. Until his death, he maintained a keenness of mind that made him an able jurist.

Once when several sessions of superior court were going on at the same time in Raleigh, the elderly judge sat on one of the benches. Judge B. T. Falls, presiding in another of the Raleigh sessions, invited him to dine with him one noon, and together they walked into a steak house where a beautiful young blonde maintained the cash register.

The elder judge smoked the girl over and when they reached their table, he said in jest to Judge Falls, "You know, Buzz, I'd give a bale of cotton to get in bed with that," and he nodded toward the pretty girl.

They dined in pleasant conversation, and the older judge had forgotten about the bale of cotton when they approached the cash register to pay their checks. The same pretty lass stood behind the register, and when Judge Falls handed her his check, he said to her, "Young lady, do you know what this white-headed old goat said about you when he came in? He said he'd give a bale of cotton to get in bed with you."

The girl stood her ground. She looked at the judge and asked, "Well, what's a bale of cotton selling for these days?"

Matter of Opinion

Robert McMillan has earned a reputation over the years of being one of the outstanding criminal defense lawyers in North Carolina. Just after he was assigned to represent a defendant confined in the Wake County jail, the defendant made a dramatic escape from the fifth-floor jail.

He was apprehended later, and under questioning, gave as his reason for escaping the fact that he did not like the "inexperienced lawyers in the indigent defense program" and that he broke out of jail to find himself a good lawyer.

A Case of Negligence

As in the courtroom, there are great moments of levity in the classrooms of the nation's law schools. A professor at the University of North Carolina law school attempted one afternoon to set the factual background of a particular case before the usual grueling Socratic method on the law began.

The case involved the construction of a bridge, and at question was whether the bridge had been constructed in accordance with the proper procedures necessary to produce a safe structure.

The city commissioning the construction of the bridge thought the bridge to be unsafe, and in the professor's words, "sued the contractors for negligent erection."

Flip of a Coin

Raleigh Attorney Sidney S. Eagles, Jr., sitting in Wake County Superior Court listening to the calling of the motion and arraignment calendar, was surprised to hear the name of a defendant whom he had been appointed to represent in district court on several misdemeanor charges which had not yet come to trial.

He was about to rise and inform Judge James H. Pou Bailey that he had been appointed in those earlier cases but to his knowledge he did not represent the young man in the case at hand, when Howard Manning, Jr., another attorney, stood and acknowledged that he had been appointed to represent the young man in similar cases in superior court, but not this one.

Several other lawyers stood one by one to advise the court that they had at one time been appointed and relieved thereafter.

Eagles was on his feet, and before he could sit down again, Judge Bailey asked why he was standing.

"Your Honor," Eagles said, "I have been appointed in district court to represent this man on several misde-meanor charges."

Manning seized the opportunity to unload his case and

said, "Your Honor, since Mr. Eagles has been appointed to represent this man on several charges, and I have been appointed for just one, shouldn't Mr. Eagles have the honor of representing him on all charges?"

Judge Bailey turned to Eagles for response, and Eagles said, "Since Mr. Manning represents him on a felony charge in a higher court and I merely have been appointed to represent the man in some lesser and insignificant misdemeanor charges in the lower district court, I believe Mr. Manning's appointment should prevail."

Two or three other proposals and reasons therefor went back and forth, until finally Judge Bailey held up his hand.

"Mr. Hall," he asked of Jack Hall, the assistant district attorney who was calling the calendar for the state, "do you have a coin?"

"Yes, Your Honor, I believe I do," Hall said, fishing out a quarter.

"Flip it in the air, Mr. Hall."

He flipped it. Before it came down, Judge Bailey said, "Mr. Manning, call it."

Manning called it heads, and heads it landed.

Eagles thus won the opportunity to represent the young man in both district court and superior court, and the superior court case is still referred to as the case Eagles "won" on the flip of a coin.

Good Advice

H. W. Zimmerman, Jr., of Lexington, was sworn in as solicitor of the Twenty-second Solicitorial District in 1971. Done in open court before all the assembled attorneys, defendants, jurors, and spectators, the formalities made

Zimmerman a bit nervous.

When the ceremony was concluded, the court suggested that Zimmerman make a short speech. The new solicitor set out the fact that he was young and inexperienced and would need all the help he could get.

From the bench then came this sage advice: "Mr. Solicitor, I have always found that there is one principle in life which, if followed, would help you out tremendously, and that is: Just do the best you can, and let it all hang out."

Turning the Tables

Superior Court Judge Henry Grady was one of the most distinguished and commanding-looking jurists in North Carolina. His hair was snow white, his build erect, and his mind sharp as a tack.

Judge Grady held court well into his eighties before the North Carolina state legislature, in its infinite wisdom, made it mandatory that judges retire from the bench at seventy-two, thus depriving our courts of some of their most able men because of mere numbers.

Late in his career, Judge Grady was assigned court in Pittsboro one term, and on a Monday morning, after oversleeping, he sped toward that town in his wife's automobile, which, of course, bore no judicial license plate.

After several miles, he looked in his rear-view mirror, and saw the thing that most motorists dread—the flashing blue light of a state highway patrolman.

"Shame! Shame!" Judge Grady admonished himself. "Here you are, a superior court judge, arrested for speeding!"

Putting his mind in high gear, he swiftly thought, "How can I get out of this situation?"

A light dawned. He knew exactly what to do.

He slammed on the brakes, swerved off the highway, and skidded to a stop in a cloud of swirling dust. The patrolman pulled in behind him.

Before the officer could get out of his car, Judge Grady dashed to the patrol car and commanded, "Roll down your window!"

The officer complied.

"Young man," the judge snapped, "I've been watching you in my mirror for three or four miles and I have never seen a car driven so recklessly! I am Judge Grady and I'm going to Pittsboro to hold court. You follow me to the courthouse and radio your sergeant to meet us there so we can have a talk about your driving."

The old judge didn't give the patrolman a chance to say a word. He sprinted back to his car and drove off. The officer followed.

When the judge parked at the courthouse, the officer parked beside him. Grady walked over to the patrol car and held out his hand.

"Young man," he said, "I want you to know that your driving improved one thousand percent on the way into town. Just cancel that call to your sergeant and forget about it."

The patrolman thanked the judge profusely and even helped him carry his bag and books into the courthouse.

Last Question

Wherever North Carolina Secretary of State Thad Eure goes, people remark about his youthful appearance.

A few years ago, Ronald Stephen Patterson, a Hayesville attorney, held the position of securities examiner for the secretary of state, and often traveled with Mr. Eure.

One evening in Mt. Airy where Eure was scheduled to address a group of concerned citizens on a matter of vital importance, Patterson went to the refreshment stand for a cold drink before Eure spoke.

Patterson struck up a conversation with a man standing near the concession stand, and before he knew it the man swung the conversation around to Thad Eure's youthful appearance.

One thing led to another, and the man asked Patterson, "How old do you think I am?"

Never an expert at age guessing, Patterson stepped back, scrutinized the man carefully, and said, "I would say you are fifty-five years old."

"Nope," the man laughed, "but I thank you. I'm seventy-two."

Patterson, then twenty-eight years old and not to be outdone, put the question back to the man. "How old do you think I am?" he asked.

The man studied him for a moment or two, and said, "You are forty-two years old."

To this day, Patterson has not asked anyone else to guess his age.

Sufficient Identification

In early 1981, Marilyn Hensley was hired as court reporter for the Thirtieth Judicial District. A lovely young lady both in personality and appearance, she was quickly nicknamed "Monroe."

Shortly thereafter, I arraigned a man in Haywood County Superior Court on a charge of giving a worthless check in the amount of $2,000 to a used car dealer in Waynesville. The defendant was from South Carolina. He had given the check on a South Carolina bank.

Shortly before the noon recess, the man entered a plea of guilty, and the judge told him to return at two o'clock for sentencing.

The judge, Monroe, and I went to lunch. At the table, she said, "You know, I can't feel too sorry for that car dealer who took a check on an out-of-state bank from a perfect stranger and let him leave with the car."

We said nothing.

"Why, sometimes when I come to court," she continued, "and forget to bring any money for lunch, I have to show them everything I've got to get a five-dollar check cashed."

Grinning, the judge said, "Monroe, any time you want to present that identification, I'll be glad to cash your check."

9 • *Disorderly Conduct*

First Things First

A young attorney had been practicing about a year, struggling and scraping to make ends meet, when a spinster woman in her middle fifties came into his office with respect to the disposition of her estate upon her death.

She advised the attorney that she did not believe in banks, nor in wills, and that she had $10,000 in cash savings which she would like to dispose of.

Bashfully, she told the attorney that she had always wanted a young man to visit her and that she likewise wanted to have one of the finest funerals that money could buy.

She extracted the $10,000 from her purse and handed it to the attorney, instructing him that on the next Saturday he should find a very fine, handsome young man to come to her home and visit her from noon until two o'clock, and that he should give this young man $3,000 of the money.

The other $7,000, she said, was to be retained for an appropriate burial service when she died.

Mulling over this unusual request, the attorney told his

wife about it at dinner that evening.

The wife remarked that $3,000 would certainly come in handy for them. "You are young," she said, "and very handsome. Why don't you visit your client from noon to two on Saturday, and we can keep the money?"

They hashed it over until they thought it was a great idea!

"And while you're there," she said, "I can get some things done around town."

"But I'll need the car to get to her house," the lawyer said.

"Oh, that's no problem," said his wife. "I'll drop you at noon and pick you up at two o'clock."

On Saturday, she drove him to the woman's home and let him out at noon. At two p.m. sharp, she drove up to the woman's home again. All the windows were closed and the blinds drawn.

She waited five minutes and her husband did not come out. She blew the horn—several times.

Finally, an upstairs window opened and her husband shouted down to her, "Come back Monday, honey; she's going to let the county bury her!"

Amnesia Victim

Don't ever think that Junior doesn't soak up everything you say, or that he will hesitate to use what he learns when occasion demands.

Bob Lacey is a district court judge. In Marshall, during pretrial conferences, the talk drifted around to children, and Lacey told Buck Talman and some other attorneys how his own six-year-old son tried to get out of going to school one day.

The young man had a friend who had just had his tonsils removed. Apparently his circle had been discussing the operation.

Mrs. Lacey went in to get her son up and get him ready for school.

"Don't touch me," the lad said. "I've got this huge lump in my throat, and I won't be able to go to school today."

"Open your mouth," said Mrs. Lacey, "and let me see it."

"I can't," said young Lacey. "It's invisible, and highly contagious. You'll catch it." He learned some pretty big words from his daddy.

Mrs. Lacey told him his ruse wouldn't do, that he must get up and go to school. So the boy went through the influenza routine, and then he had the stomachache. One by one, he tried various ailments, but his mother refused to accept them.

She became exasperated, however, and sent the boy downstairs to see his father.

On the way down, young Lacey decided an illness wouldn't work any better on his father than on his mother, so he came up with a new one.

He'd heard his father talk about drunks in the courtroom, so he opened the door and staggered into the room where his father sat.

"I can't go to school today," he announced. "I'm too drunk!"

Judge Lacey lowered the newspaper he was reading, and fixed his son with his sternest judicial stare.

"Huh-oh," the boy thought, "if I don't come up with something better than that, I've had it."

The judge continued to hold him with a silent stare, and the boy stared back.

"Now I've got amnesia," he said. "Do I know you?"

New Identity

One of Western North Carolina's outstanding trial lawyers and his secretary of long standing, a woman with whom he had never engaged in hanky-panky, flew to Kansas City on business.

From the airport the two went directly to the hotel where the secretary had made reservations, and the clerk said that through computer error their adjoining rooms had already been filled.

The lawyer was enraged and threatened to sue when the clerk told him that there was, in fact, only one room vacant in the entire hotel.

"It has two beds," the clerk said, "and we will be glad to hang a blanket between the beds to give you some privacy."

There was nothing to do but take the room, and the attorney and secretary vowed to make the best of it.

After dinner, they went to the room to retire. The air-conditioner was broken, so the attorney opened wide the window, and the two retired in separate beds.

About midnight they awakened. A storm howled outside and the room was freezing cold.

"I'm cold," said the secretary, "will you please close the window?"

The attorney thought a moment and said, "I have a better idea. How would you like to be my wife tonight?"

"Oh, yes," she breathed, "I'd love to."

"Then get up," he ordered, "and close the window."

Switcheroo!

Thad D. Bryson, Jr., able attorney, solicitor, and superior court judge for many years, was a tale-teller who was prone to embellish. Having a great sense of humor, he was also very adept at pulling pranks on his friends.

Once, Judge Bryson and two of the greatest mountain men ever raised in the Smokies, Uncle Mark Cathey and Granville Calhoun, went on an all-night fox hunt, and carried with them a liberal quantity of snakebite medicine.

Uncle Mark and Mr. Calhoun were both in their eighties at the time, but both were more than able to participate in all aspects of the hunt.

The three hiked to the top of a tall mountain in Swain County, turned loose their dogs, built a good campfire, and proceeded to warm their innards with 160-proof.

About midnight, with all feeling good, having heard several good races from the dogs, and filled to the gills with snakebite juice, the three decided it was time for some sleep.

Both Cathey and Calhoun were equipped with full sets of hinged false teeth, which they had to remove before settling down for the night. Each placed his teeth on a different stump and went to sleep.

When their snores resounded from the campsite, Thad switched their teeth.

Next morning, Thad woke up to loud swearing. There sat Uncle Mark on his stump trimming a set of teeth with his pocket knife, and Mr. Calhoun on his stump hollering that his teeth had stretched during the night.

As good sports as Thad knew them to be, he still didn't tell this tale until after both were gone.

Mr. Lyndon's Chauffeur

Everybody in Jackson County knew, admired, and respected Lyndon McKee, whom we all called "Mr. Lyndon." In the 1930s, Mr. Lyndon had a large and corpulent black man named Bob who was a live-in valet and chauffeur.

Occasionally Bob took a weekend off, and before one of those weekends Mr. Lyndon gave him a half-gallon of corn whiskey.

On Monday morning, Bob dragged himself back to Mr. Lyndon's house, much the worse for wear.

Mr. Lyndon's eyes twinkled when he saw Bob's condition.

"Bob," he asked, "how was the whiskey?"

"That whiskey was jes' right, Mr. Lyndon," Bob replied, trying to hold open his eyes. "If it had been any better you would have kept it, and if it had been any worse I couldn't have drunk it."

She Wouldn't Go!

Dr. Stanley McQuade is a most unusual, versatile individual. He holds degrees in both law and medicine. For several years he practiced medicine in Bryson City, the seat of Swain County, and as most small-town doctors do, he had patients from almost all of the surrounding communities.

Among other things, he served as an anesthesiologist for other physicians practicing surgery, and thus was at those controls, administering the anesthesia, when an elderly woman from Robbinsville underwent surgery in

188

Bryson City.

The operation was an unqualified success and the woman went home singing lavish praises of the physicians who had served her. Talking to a friend about her surgery, she praised her surgeon and several other doctors, then said, "I can't speak too highly of that new doctor, Dr. McQuade, in Bryson City. He specialized in anesthesiology—and he certainly knows what he is doing!"

Her friend, a devout Baptist, was not at all impressed.

"Well," she huffed, "I would never allow anyone to treat me who doesn't believe in God!"

Here It Are!

Attorney Buck Talman found his backyard flooded. He searched the yard for the source of water but failed to find it.

In a hurry to get to work, Buck telephoned a plumber who said he would send two men over right away.

"Tell them," Buck said, "to dig up the pipes and fix them. The yard's beginning to look like Lake James."

Buck spent the morning in court, then went home for lunch. The yard was still flooded, and two men had dug several large holes in the lawn. "We haven't found it yet," one said, "but we will—if we have to dig up the whole blasted yard."

Buck's three-year-old son, Wesley Fleming Talman III, appeared. He asked his father what the men were doing.

"They're digging holes," Buck said, "to find a water leak, but they can't find it."

Wesley marched over to the side of the yard and

extracted a hose from a large pile of pine needles. A steady stream of water came from the hose.

"Here it are," he said. He had filled his wading pool the afternoon before and couldn't figure how to turn off the hose.

The two men glared at Buck. They packed their tools and left.

But they said they'd send a bill.

One Way or Another!

A young woman from Macon County went on a date with her boy friend, and during the course of the evening they engaged in such a heated argument that he called her a bitch and used other profane language.

The next morning the girl swore out a warrant for the young man for his use of profane language.

When the case came before the court, the judge asked her, "What is this case about?"

"Your Honor," said the young woman, "this man called me a bitch and used a lot of other bad language in my presence."

The judge gave the young man a tongue-lashing he wouldn't forget, and cautioned him never to use profane language to the lady again. "And especially," the judge said, "you are never again to call her a bitch."

He fined the man fifty dollars and costs and warned him that if he ever came back before his court on similar charges he would "throw the book" at him.

"Your Honor," the young man asked, "can I ask you a question?"

"Yes, you may. What is it?"

"Can a person be fined for thinking, Your Honor?"

"Of course not," the judge snapped.

"In that case," said the young man, "I still think she's a bitch."

Who Could Ask for More?

Around 1976 a certain judge held a special session of Jackson County Superior Court. He brought his lovely wife with him to enjoy the beauty of the mountains.

During the session, my wife Jane and I had the Judge and his wife come to our home for dinner. We spent a wonderful evening talking about our days together when I was in the legislature.

Several times that evening, the judge made reference to how wonderful his wife was. He even got to bragging a bit.

"You know, Buck," said he, "I'm the luckiest man in North Carolina. I have a beautiful wife; she's young, oversexed, and has a brother who owns a liquor store in South Carolina. Who could ask for more from just one woman!"

The Judge and the Women

Several years ago, a certain superior court judge came to Murphy to hold a term of court for Cherokee County. If there has ever been a male counterpart of Carrie Nations, it was this judge: He had never touched alcohol in any shape or fashion. He was such a teetotaler that it was said he never allowed his wife to use vanilla extract in her cakes.

At that time, Duke's Lodge was a fabulous, rustic lodge about five miles out of Murphy, and on Sunday nights before court on Monday, all the lawyers, the judge, and the solicitor gathered there around five in the afternoon, set up a bar on the porch, and proceeded to imbibe a little before tackling one of Duke's thick steaks.

As solicitor, I had made reservations for the judge at a certain motel, and I waited for him there. Five o'clock passed and the judge hadn't showed. I waited until six o'clock and the judge still wasn't there. Knowing the crowd that had gathered at Duke's, I figured if I didn't get there soon, all the pre-meal stimulus would be gone, so I left a deputy sheriff to wait for the judge and made my way to the lodge.

A half-hour later, up drove the deputy with the judge. I introduced him to all the lawyers and court officials, observing him all the time casting suspicious glances toward the bar.

Knowing his lack of affinity for strong drink, but out of courtesy, I asked if I could mix him anything.

Drawing himself to his full five feet, six inches, he looked me straight in the eye and replied: "No, thank you; I never touch the stuff—but you boys go ahead and drink, and I'll handle the women."

The Woman Baiter

Blaine Stalcup, sheriff of Cherokee County, is relatively harmless to women, but he loves to kid with them. All the good ladies in and around Murphy know he is harmless and pay no attention to his advances.

I was holding court in that beautiful marble courthouse

in Murphy one day and Blaine asked me to go with him to lunch.

We had to stop by the clerk's office, and in it was a table about four feet high over which people paid traffic tickets. A winsome little girl wearing a micro-miniskirt was leaning over the table, her bottom shining, talking to the clerk.

Blaine was a couple of steps ahead of me and as he passed through the partition beyond the table, he reached out and gave the girl a little pat on her fanny.

He disappeared inside the partition, leaving me standing there looking at the girl with my mouth open. When she saw no one but me, and me a stranger, she gave me a resounding slap on the cheek.

She got away with it, too. What could I say?—except that I owed Blaine one.

Bad Shape

Jim Johnson used to run a funeral home. His wife was a teetotaler, and when Jim got drunk, which was with regularity, she took him to the local jail where she had made arrangements for facilities to sober him up.

One Saturday night she loaded him in the car, passed out and sick, and drove him to the jail where the sheriff put him in a cell where he could sober up overnight.

Early the next morning, the sheriff went up to let Jim out and Jim said, "Sheriff, ain't you got something for a sick man?"—meaning, of course, he needed a drink and needed it badly.

The sheriff said, "Jim, don't you feel too good?"

"Hell," Jim replied, "I've buried people who felt better than me."

Life's Little Necessities

For many years one of our mountain cities had only one general mercantile store in town and it specialized in *everything.* If the general store didn't have it, it just wasn't to be found!

In those days, the women in the remote areas birthed their babies at home. Diapers as such were not sold, but rather diaper cloth could be procured at the general store, cut from a bolt to the proper size and hemmed for the purpose intended.

Canada Township was a very isolated section, accessible only by a narrow dirt road, infrequently used except by residents and on infrequent occasions by others to procure the fine moonshine whiskey for which Canada was known.

Once, when a woman had a "granny scrape," the baby arrived early, so early in fact that she hadn't had the time to buy her diaper cloth.

The father sent his long, lanky, sixteen-year-old son to town to pick up ten yards of such cloth. The lad walked all the way, and when he strode into the general store, he was greeted by the saleslady who for thirty years oversaw the dry goods department.

The boy, bashful as all getout, walked around the store for some time, spotted the diaper cloth, but when asked by the saleslady if she could help him, was too shy to ask for the item.

Sensing a sale, but after a number of negative attempts, the saleslady went to the owner and told him what was happening.

"Send the boy back here," he said.

In a few moments, the young man entered the office. He was still sensitive about being waited upon by a woman, and when the owner asked if he wanted to buy something, the boy said yes, but he hadn't made up his mind yet.

Knowing that some of the Canada folks, even those this young man's age, used a little white lightning to bolster their courage now and then, the owner pulled a half-gallon of spirits out of his desk and asked the boy if he'd like a little drink.

"I guess I could take a little swaller," the boy replied, and poured himself half a water glass and downed it without chaser or blink of an eye.

After a few minutes, the owner observed a flush come to the boy's cheeks, and he asked if he had made up his mind yet.

"Not yet," the boy stammered, "but maybe if I could have just another little bit."

Soon the owner observed that the young man was losing his inhibitions, so he asked again if he knew what he wanted yet.

"Believe I do," said the young man, and quickly exited the office.

The saleslady was waiting. "Can I help you?" she asked.

"Hell, yes, you can," the boy said. "I want ten yards of diaper cloth."

"Of course," said the saleslady. "Do you want bleached or unbleached?"

"Don't give a damn which way it is," the lad said, "just so's it'll hold what it's supposed to hold."

Fred's Sick Mule

Typical of our mountain sheriffs, Fred Holcombe of Jackson County knows his people, is firm and tough when the need arises, humble and fair to everyone, honest in everything he does—and loves mules.

That peculiarity will go with him to his grave: He simply loves mules and would never be without one.

He once went to a mule sale in Kentucky and bought what he thought was the finest mule he had ever seen. He loaded it into his truck and drove happily home.

Next morning, before daylight, Fred couldn't wait any longer to check on his prize mule. He went to the barn, and by lantern light saw his mule lying flat on the ground, breathing hard, panting, and groaning.

Scared the mule was going to die, Fred jumped in his car and sped to the veterinarian's house, waked the good doctor and told him the symptoms of his mule.

The vet thought a minute and said, "I know what's wrong with your mule, Fred. It's something that's going around, and nothing to be alarmed about."

From a cabinet he withdrew six rectal suppositories and gave them to Fred. "Insert one of these in that mule's rectum every four hours," he said, "and in twenty-four hours your mule should be as good as new."

Fred sped back home, went straight to the barn, and found the mule in the same shape it had been in when he left. He walked around the mule four or five times, inspecting it closely, finally stopping at its head. He shook his finger in its face and said, "Mule, I'm gonna walk around you one more time, and if I don't find your rectum, I'm gonna ram one of these up your butt!"

Age Really Is Relative

A woman of approximately eighty years, who appeared to have seen her better days, kept an appointment with her doctor to have some recurrent stomach pains checked out.

The doctor ran a routine examination, then spent a half-hour or more giving her various tests to confirm his suspicions. He then told her to get dressed and wait for him in his private office.

Fifteen minutes later he walked into his office shaking his head.

"Mrs. Jones," he said, "I have some rather surprising news for you—and the only way I know to tell you is without elaboration. Mrs. Jones, you are pregnant!"

Mrs. Jones was aghast. "Doctor," she said, "that just couldn't be! Not at my age! It's an impossibility!"

"Nevertheless," said the doctor, "I have run every test available, and each was positive. There is no question: You are a walking miracle. Mrs. Jones, you really are pregnant!"

"You are certain, aren't you, doctor?"

"Absolutely. There is no question."

"Then may I telephone my husband?"

"Of course," said the doctor. "Use my phone. Tell him the good news."

Mrs. Jones dialed her telephone number, and her ninety-year-old husband answered the phone.

In a voice loud and clear, mincing no words, Mrs. Jones emphatically announced, "You bald-headed old goat— you've got me pregnant!"

There was a short silence, and then her husband whispered, "Who is this?"

A Charge of Rape

A barking dog can get a man charged with rape—if circumstances happen to work against him.

That's what happened, in a roundabout way, to a man of sixty-nine who lived peacefully in an Asheville neighborhood.

He had never had trouble with any of his neighbors. He had always made a practice of getting along with them, of going the extra mile if he had to, or certainly of meeting them more than half way.

The woman across the road began collecting dogs. She had no husband, no children, only several dogs of various pedigree—and various vocal tone.

They barked at night, some high-toned, some low-pitched, all loud. They barked and barked, and finally began to drive the old man up the wall. He complained to the woman, but she was protective of her dogs and told the man to mind his own business and let her dogs alone.

They continued to bark at night, disturbing his sleep, sometimes robbing him of a full night's sleep. Not knowing where to turn, he checked the records and discovered that the woman had enough dogs to qualify for kennel status, but she couldn't have a kennel in the city.

She was forced to divest herself of some of her dogs, and that really angered her. She put her vicious tongue against the man, gossiping about him throughout the neighborhood. Some of the things she said, though untrue, enraged the man's next-door neighbors, and their youngsters salted the man's lawn and killed his grass.

When he set out with a flashlight at night, trying to get evidence against the boys and have them apprehended, the neighbor told him he was a madman.

Now he was being sniped at from across the street and from next door, and he was sniping back in both directions.

The next-door neighbor put an ad in the paper that a garage sale would be held at the old man's address, and when numerous carloads of people showed up for the sale, the old man told them the paper got the address wrong, that the sale was next door.

That night, he put his hat on his wife's dressmaking mannequin and stood it next to his next-door neighbor's window, and it frightened the woman within an inch of her life. The next day, when the man went out to work in his yard, the neighbor turned her hose on him.

He discovered that his neighbor's rock garden extended onto his property and put up a chain link fence through the garden. She retaliated by killing all the flowers in the garden on his side of the fence.

Her kids began making nuisance calls to his telephone. One would call, put a handkerchief over the phone, and say, "This is the Ku Klux Klan. We're going to kill you."

He complained to the telephone company, and the phone people put a device on his phone to trace the threatening calls. The old man knew where the calls were coming from, however, and more than wanting to stop them, he wanted to use them in another way against the neighbor.

When the neighbor kids called his number, the device on his telephone froze their line open as long as his receiver was off the hook.

When they called, he left the receiver off and went out on the porch to listen. Soon he heard one of the neighbor kids say, "Something's wrong with this phone."

"What is it?" their mother asked.

"I don't know," the kid said. "I can't get a dial tone."

"Go somewhere and call the phone company," she said.

The old man sat on his porch until he saw the telephone repairman pull into the neighbor's yard. He went inside, replaced the receiver, and went back out.

He heard the telephone repairman say, "There's nothing wrong with this phone. It works okay."

The old man consulted an attorney who told him that he could legally fight fire with fire, as long as he didn't step across a certain line.

"I remember a case," the attorney said, "in which a man's neighbor continually had loud parties until one in the morning, and when the man complained, they laughed at him. So the man got a recorder and taped the noise from one of the parties. He played the tape in his front yard in the wee hours of the night, turning the tape player up full blast."

The old man thought about that for a while. The whole thing, he knew, had started with the barking dogs across the street—and they still barked at night.

He bought a megaphone and sat up until well after midnight, barking back at the dogs. The woman came to him the next day and said, "I would appreciate it if you would quit barking."

"Sorry," the old man said. "I've got as much right to bark as your dogs do."

They discovered, however, that they could talk to one another, and they reached a compromise. She put up her dogs at night, and he quit barking through his megaphone.

But that didn't appease the woman next door.

He bought a Doberman, a huge, ugly, mean one.

One afternoon when the lady next door came out to

walk her lap dog, the old man stood with his Doberman on a leash. The little dog got loose and tore across the man's lawn charging the Doberman.

The man uttered a single command to the Doberman, "Get him!" The Doberman began to strain and buck and growl and bark.

But the old man hadn't counted on the woman's reaction. She charged across the street, threw a crushing football block on the old man and the Doberman, and rescued her poodle.

Then she ran to the courthouse and took out a warrant for the old man, charging him with rape.

That's how he wound up in court, answering a rape charge that began with five barking dogs.

He was also charged with resisting arrest. When the police came for him, he grabbed a pillar on his front porch and held on for dear life. The officer had to pry him loose, and charged him with resisting arrest.

Under oath, the woman testified that the sixty-nine-year-old man tried to rape her. She said when she threw the body block on the old man and the Doberman that he pulled her down, tore at her clothing, and tried to rape her.

"Did he ever turn loose of the Doberman?" asked Joe Reynolds, the defense attorney.

"No, sir, he never did," the woman said. "He held onto the dog."

"Your Honor," Reynolds said, "we concede that this man may have resisted arrest by holding on to his front porch, but we submit that it would have been impossible for him to hold on to a mad Doberman who was pitching and bucking and growling and barking—and try to rape this woman at the same time. That would be a physical impossibility for a thirty-year-old man, let alone a man of sixty-nine."

The judge took one look at the wizened old man, another at the thirty-year-old woman who had filed the charges—and dismissed all charges.

Here, Have One!

Junius Bubble was an outstanding private eye in Asheville. He loved gumshoe work, even though many of the cases he got were those in which a wife hired him to follow her husband, or vice versa. He kept waiting for the big one—one like you see every day on television.

When it came, it struck unexpectedly, but with a decided theatrical twist.

A husband hired him to follow his wife, and in the course of a few weeks Junius followed her to the same motel every Friday afternoon where she met the same man and spent a couple of hours with him, hidden away in a motel room.

One Friday, the man brought a friend, another man, and the three of them entered the motel room and stayed two hours.

On the following Friday, Junius went to the motel manager and asked if he could bug the room that the woman and her friends would use that afternoon.

"Under one condition," the motel manager said.

"What's that?" Junius asked.

"That you let me listen in."

They agreed, and Junius wired the room for sound. He set up the receivers in an adjoining room, and when the wife arrived with her two friends and entered the room,

Junius and the motel manager crept into the next room and put on their headphones.

They heard a couple of shoes hit the floor, then two more, then the woman said, "Give me a cigarette."

Neither man said anything, but Junius and the manager could hear the swish of dropping clothes.

"I want a cigarette," the woman said.

"Pull 'em off, honey," said one of the men.

"Gimme a cigarette!"

"I don't have a cigarette," one of the men answered. "Take 'em off."

"I don't take nothing off," the female voice said, "till I get a cigarette."

"I don't have one, either," said the other male voice. "Come on, let's get on with it."

"We don't get on with nothing," said the woman, "until I get a smoke."

"Aw, honey . . . ."

"GIVE ME A CIGARETTE!"

"I don't have a cigarette. Now, dammit, get in that bed!"

"Go to hell."

"TAKE 'EM OFF!"

"GIMME A CIGARETTE!"

Junius looked at his watch. Ten minutes had passed. He looked at the manager, who raised his eyebrows. Slowly, Junius removed his headphones, rose from his chair, and went silently out the door.

He stepped to the door of the adjoining room, knocked, and when one of the men cracked the door and peeped out, Junius calmly shook a cigarette out of his own pack, handed it to the man, and said, "Here, give her one of mine."

Marcellus "Buck" Buchanan

Marcellus "Buck" Buchanan was born and reared in Sylva, North Carolina, where he presently resides. He and his wife Jane have two grown children, Mark and Christina.

Buck's sojourns away from his native mountains have all been temporary—to the University of North Carolina at Chapel Hill to obtain his legal education, and to Raleigh to represent Jackson County in the North Carolina House of Representatives for three terms in the 1950s.

Since 1967, he has been the Superior Court Solicitor for North Carolina's Thirtieth Judicial District which is comprised of Cherokee, Clay, Graham, Haywood, Jackson, Macon, and Swain counties. Buck also served as Democratic Committee Chairman of Jackson County. His travels and experiences throughout North Carolina have given him ample opportunity to add to his stock of humorous and human-interest anecdotes. *Disorder in the Court!* is Buchanan's first book, but he's long had a local reputation as a memorable storyteller.

Bob Terrell

Bob Terrell is also a native of Sylva, North Carolina, and a graduate of Western Carolina University. He is the father of three sons—Bobby, Zeke, and Jake. Bob and his wife Vivian make their home in Asheville.

Terrell joined the staff of *The Asheville Citizen-Times* in 1949 as a sports writer. Since then he's been sports editor, news editor, and is now associate editor of the *Citizen-Times*. But it is as a daily column writer and after-dinner speaker that Bob has earned his reputation as a chronicler of Western North Carolina's fun and foibles.

Columns soon emerged as books, mostly written just for entertainment, such as *Fun Is Where You Find It! A Touch of Terrell*, and *Old Gold*. This latest book, *Disorder in the Court!*, brings us more of the same fun and foibles, this time with an emphasis on courtroom antics as witnessed by Bob and his cohort, Marcellus Buchanan.